Roger Federer: The Inspiring Story of One of Tennis' Greatest Legends

An Unauthorized Biography

By: Clayton Geoffreys

Visit my website at www.claytongeoffreys.com
Cover photo by Tatiana Kulitat is licensed under CC BY 2.0 / modified from original

Table of Contents

Foreword

Roger Federer, Rafael Nadal, and Novak Djokovic have dominated the game of tennis over the last decade. Each player has had his own period of dominance, but Roger Federer is arguably the greatest tennis player to ever play the game. The reason for this statement being that as of early 2017, he has won eighteen Grand Slam titles, the most in history for a male tennis player. Aside from his sheer dominance on the court, Federer has also set an example for future generations of players on what it means to be an all-around class act. When he ultimately retires from the game, he will be dearly missed. Thank you for purchasing *Roger Federer: The Inspiring Story of One of Tennis' Greatest Legends*. In this unauthorized biography, we will learn Roger Federer's incredible life story and impact on the game of tennis. Hope you enjoy and if you do, please do not forget to leave a review!

Also, check out my website at claytongeoffreys.com to join my exclusive list where I let you know about my latest books. To thank you for your purchase, you can go to my site to download a free copy of *33 Life Lessons: Success Principles, Career Advice & Habits of Successful People*. In the book, you'll learn from some of the greatest thought leaders of different industries on what it takes to become successful and how to live a great life.

Cheers,

Clayton Geoffreys

Visit me at www.claytongeoffreys.com

Introduction

There are four things for which Switzerland is globally renowned: Chocolate, precision timepieces, neutrality, and Roger Federer. The last allows the Swiss people to blissfully ignore the third when it comes to discussing where the superstar tennis player ranks in the sport's pantheon.

Federer has an enjoyed a playing career that is at the sunset of a second decade, and his recent recovery from knee surgery and Renaissance to win the Australian Open in January 2017 shows that the Swiss maestro still has something left in his bag of tricks, even at age 35.

His 18 Grand Slam singles titles are the most of any player in the Open Era. That number is more impressive considering that his career intersected the sport's history at a time where Rafael Nadal and Novak Djokovic tied for second and fourth place in that category with 14 and 12, respectively.

These three players have had a stranglehold on major titles for nearly a generation, winning the Australian Open, French Open, Wimbledon, and the U.S. Open a combined 44 times dating to Federer's first Wimbledon crown in summer of 2003. But it is the elegant Federer who currently stands above the gritty Nadal and the jack-of-all-surfaces Djokovic, due in large part to his metronome-like consistency at an elite level for more than a decade.

On the path to becoming arguably the greatest of all time in his sport, Federer's rise was one seen in the distance, starting with his play in juniors. He had to mature from petulant teenager to talented and promising young player on the ATP Tour. Federer then had to absorb match and life lessons from his peers to become a better player.

And since the summer following his first victory at the all-England club, Federer's place in tennis lore has come by way of reaction and evolution. He has honed his already finely tuned all-around game and enhanced it with strategy. That often kept him one step ahead of the chasing pack, though now in the autumn of his playing days, it is helping him try to emerge from it.

This is the story of Roger Federer, the man who likely will be tennis' all-time greatest player when he retires.

Chapter 1: Early Life and Childhood

Roger Federer was born August 8, 1981, in Basel. He was the younger child in the family, 22 months junior to his sister Diana. Roger's parents, Robert and the former Lynette Durand, met in South Africa as co-workers for Ciba, a chemical company (1).

Robert Federer was born in Berneck, Switzerland, a village that is so close to the Austrian border and Rhine River that many of its citizens speak German. At the age of 20, Robert Federer felt the desire to see the world, and it took him to South Africa, which was a commercial hub for foreign companies. Ciba was located in Kempton Park, which is on the outskirts of Johannesburg, and is considered a suburb of the country's largest city. Like Robert Federer, Durand had a sense of adventure and a want of travel. She was multilingual and had hopes of visiting Europe and England to retrace her father's steps as a soldier in World War II (2).

The two saw each other for the first time in the company cafeteria in 1970 and eventually became a couple. By this point, Robert Federer had just begun to take up tennis as a hobby and sold Durand on the sport's merits. The two played regularly at the Swiss Club in Johannesburg, and their relationship grew.

But by 1973, the couple had moved back to Switzerland, in part due to Robert's wanderlust. There was an uneasy transition to the Nordic country for Durand given the tiny size of Switzerland and his whole new outlook. In South Africa, apartheid was the law of the land, though it did not affect the couple (3).

The country they worked for continued to play a vital role in their lives and shared hobby of tennis. Ciba sponsored a tennis club in a suburb of Basel called Allschwil, and the Federers became members. Lynette, who played field hockey as a young woman and had arguably as much athletic prowess as Robert, honed her game to the point that she was a member of a club winning team (4).

Her love of the sport led her to take on a role as a junior coach, and she was an active participant in club tournament activities. Robert was no slouch on the tennis court himself, showing enough skill to be ranked at a regional level. Though the couple added golf to their list of hobby sports, it was quickly apparent that young Roger was enamored with tennis.

He would tag along with his parents to the club, and once Roger was given a racket after his third birthday, things took off. He quickly showed a considerable amount of athletic coordination, but he also had a volatile temper that came with a very competitive nature.

Roger Federer was headstrong from a very early age, sometimes out of curiosity, but mainly with a clear purpose to find out what limits were set upon him. Though highly energetic, he would quickly disengage if he lost interest. It was also clear early on that he was gifted athletically and was a natural for sports. His favorites were football (soccer), team handball, basketball, and table tennis, in addition to tennis (5).

Roger's parents were keen to let their son figure out what he liked and did not like for sports, but they also realized they had to rein in his somewhat combative personality. They enrolled him in the local soccer club in Basel mainly so that he could learn to be a teammate and team player (6).

The Federer family was very typical for Switzerland: middle class and not lacking for anything. When compared with Novak Djokovic's upbringing in war-torn Serbia, Federer's childhood comes across as idyllic. Roger's relationship with his older sister Diana was a normal one between siblings, in particular with a younger brother. Roger would be the ham and playfully torment her with pranks and ways to steal attention from her friends (7).

Though he played other sports, it was evident that tennis was going to be Federer's love. He took an instant shine to Boris Becker, who spectacularly shook up the tennis world with his 1985 Wimbledon victory as a teenager who dove all over the all-England club and took home many a grass-stained pair of tennis shorts in addition to the adulation as a Grand Slam winner.

By the time Roger was in grade school, his tennis talent was already apparent. He was taking training sessions in a circuit of clubs around the Basel area and finally made a friend in Marco Chiudinelli. The two became inseparable on and off the court and were more than a handful at practice because they were usually more preoccupied with each other than learning more about their sport (8).

"We talked more than we trained," Federer recalled. "Training didn't seem too important to us. We just wanted to have a good time, and we goofed around a lot. One of us was frequently kicked off the court," (9).

The rambunctiousness of Federer revealed that he had little desire to practice, just to play. Winning and losing mattered to Federer, and little else did. That all changed in two watershed

8

moments. The first was being introduced to tennis coach Adolf Kacovsky at The Old Boys Tennis Club (10).

Kacovsky, who had fled Czechoslovakia during the Prague Spring of 1968, quickly recognized Federer as a talent and shepherded him into individual lessons. For his part, Federer proved to be a quick study and flourished under Kacovsky's guidance. It also started Federer on the path of self-belief that he could be a great tennis player, and he told his coach that he "wanted to be the best in the world" (11).

The second pivotal moment came in Federer's first competitive tennis match at the age of eight. He was double-bageled, losing 6-0, 6-0 (12). There is no score line worse in tennis. Think about that for a second. The greatest tennis player of all-time was humbled as horribly as he could be at the start of the path that provided his greatness.

The defeat sparked a fanatical work ethic in young Roger, who would seek out playing partners of all types, or hit for hours against the most formidable opponent of any burgeoning tennis player, the wall. His play improved, and so did his ranking, though he encountered another obstacle in the form of Dany Schnyder.

Schnyder, whose sister Patty was a top player on the WTA Tour, had Federer's number in the early matches between them. It took nearly ten matches for Federer to figure out how to beat Schnyder, but once he did, it became lopsided in Federer's favor (13).

The fiery work ethic that fanned Federer's competitive flames did likewise with his temper. Federer was often petulant on the court and his own worst enemy. Racquet tosses were occasional; muttering expletives was constant. It took admonishment by both Kacovsky and Federer's parents to bring his temper down to a slow boil (14).

That hard work, though, paid off by age 11 when he won his first two titles. He defeated Chiudinelli in the Swiss 12-and-under indoor championships, and then Schnyder six months later in the outdoor tournament. His success, and the juggling of two sports practice schedules, led him to finally giving up soccer so he could concentrate solely on tennis (15).

By this point, Federer was also sometimes trained by Peter Carter, a native of Australia who had a modicum of success on the ATP Tour as a top 200 player. He was also a player on the Old Boys Tennis Club satellite team and was offered a coaching position to build a mentoring program.

Carter proved to be the right coach at the right time for Federer. The Australian quickly recognized Federer's natural talent and his ability to learn easily, and Carter pitched the idea of sending Federer to Ecublens to train at the Swiss National Tennis Center to his parents (16).

At first, Federer balked at the notion, but then set himself a goal to graduate from the sports academy. He passed an entrance exam at Lake Geneva, which included a test match to gain acceptance into the sports academy for the next phase of his sport and personal growth.

Though Ecublens was only a three-hour train ride from Basel, it was an entirely different world for Federer as he stayed with a foster family while at the academy. For starters, he did not speak French, which was the default language both on and off the court. Additionally, he was still somewhat aloof and did not make too many friends while there (17).

Federer also had to go from being a big fish in a small pond to a small fish in a big one. He was now among the youngest players, and there were also bigger and better players. Federer won a national 14-and-under title, but homesickness dogged the teenager as he often counted down the hours to the train ride back to Basel to be with friends and family (18).

That loneliness eased somewhat as Roger made friends with Vincent Christinet, the youngest son of his foster family in Ecublens. But the issues that made Federer, Federer, notably the lack of interest in anything that was not tennis, were manifesting themselves concerning poor academics and a lack of discipline. But these eventually washed away as he grew more comfortable in his surroundings.

The biggest sign of progress at the academy came with a trip to the United States to participate in the 14-and-under championships at the Orange Bowl in Miami. Federer needed to qualify to enter the main draw, and he did so by not dropping a set in three victories. He then won three more matches before eventually losing in the round of 16, but the confidence gained from playing among peers considered the best in the world was highly beneficial (19).

Chapter 2: Juniors and Early Career

Now a teenager, Federer was showcasing his talent. He already had won five Swiss national titles at the 16-and-under level, so it was time to expose him to other forms of competition. Carter and fellow academy coach Reto Staubli were his teammates in the Swiss interclub's top league, and he participated in the World Youth Cup in the summer of 1996.

At that tournament, he defeated a young Australian named Lleyton Hewitt, and their paths would often cross on the ATP Tour in a battle to be the world's top-ranked player. Despite being only 15 years old, Federer had already cracked the top 100 players ranking in Switzerland, and his stature grew further by winning the 18-and-under indoor and outdoor national tournaments at the age of 16 (20).

There were no kingdoms left to conquer in Switzerland for Federer, who was the primary beneficiary of the Swiss Tennis Federation's decision to create a new national tennis center in Biel. An ultra-modern facility that had multiple surfaces and player amenities, it also made the most important personnel decision that was central to Federer: bringing Carter on board as part of its coaching staff (21).

While Federer received primarily individual coaching from Carter, former professional player Peter Lundgren also became part of that circle once the center in Biel opened. At the age of 16, Federer opted to turn professional once his mandatory schooling was complete (22).

He had the backing of his parents, but they also wanted him to make a firm commitment to being the best he could be. Finances were not much of an issue because the Swiss Tennis Federation contributed to his backing, but it proved to be an unfounded fear.

At Biel, Federer shared an apartment with Yves Allegro, who was three years his senior. Chiudinelli also moved to Biel, attracted by the siren call of the new tennis center, and the three of them were a circle of friends, focused on tennis and little else in the outside world.

Federer's international profile took off in 1998. He lost in the semifinals of the Australian Open junior singles tournament, squandering a match point in the process. He won a clay-court title in Italy, but in what could be termed a foreshadowing of his struggles for consistency on the surface, he lost in the first round of the French Open junior's tournament (23).

Federer, though, quickly bounced back by winning the Wimbledon juniors, becoming the first Swiss player to accomplish that feat since Heinz Günthardt in 1976. He also teamed Belgian Olivier Rochus to win the doubles title at the all-England club (24).

With the Wimbledon title came a wild-card entry into the Swiss Open in Gstaad the following week. It would be his first ATP Tournament, and the wild card was needed since his ranking of 702nd in the world did not qualify him for direct entry (25). Despite Federer's confidence, there were many factors against him in his professional debut.

The surface change from grass to clay would require transition and a different running style. The change in altitude from sea level at Wimbledon to over 3,000 feet at Gstaad meant that balls would travel faster and bounce higher. But most notably, the caliber of opponent would skyrocket exponentially higher.

Federer would no longer be playing against his peers in age that he was dominating in skill level. These were pros who all had a high skill level, and most were greater than the Swiss teenager was at that point.

The Swiss media were eager to learn more about the precocious Federer following his Wimbledon title, and he provided some

Grade-A material by expressing his lament of not playing on Centre Court against scheduled opponent Tommy Haas, who was ranked 41st in the world (26).

Haas, though, was forced to withdraw shortly before the start of the match because of a stomach illness. In his place was Lucas Arnold, considered a "lucky loser" from the qualifying tournament as a last-minute fill-in (27). But the Argentine had one key advantage over Federer, and that was a mastery of the clay surface.

So Federer's first match as a professional resulted in a 6-4, 6-4 loss to the 88th-ranked player on the ATP Tour (28). But there were still positives to be found the rest of the year. He was on the traveling Davis Cup team for Switzerland, which provided Stephane Oberer the opportunity to mentor young Federer.

He reached the U.S. Open junior finals, losing to David Nalbandian, but also cemented his top-three status in the junior world rankings. Federer also played his way into the quarterfinals of an ATP Tour tournament in Toulouse, France, earning more than $10,000 in prize money, but also vaulting him nearly 500 spots in the world rankings to number 396 (29).

That success resulted in a direct wild-card entry into the Swiss Indoors tournament, which meant a guaranteed payday. It also served as a homecoming since the tournament site of Jakobshalle was walking distance from the family home in Munchenstein.

But the happy ending dreams of lifting a trophy in his hometown quickly gave way to the sobering reality of having to face Andre Agassi in the first round. Still a top 10 player in the world at this point, the former world number 1 dismantled Federer in a 6-3, 6-2 victory that hardly taxed the American (30).

Like all young players, Federer had his ups and downs. After that defeat to Agassi, he was fined $100 for violating the "best effort" rule for lackluster play in a lesser tournament in Kublis, Switzerland. The fine was more than the prize money he earned with his first-round defeat; Federer owed the tournament $13 because of his actions, or inactions if you prefer (31).

But that incident also matured him. He regrouped to dominate the Swiss tennis circuit and moved on the cusp of the top 300 in the ATP rankings when his 17th birthday rolled around. His goal of being the number 1 ranked juniors player at the end of 1998 moved closer to fruition after winning the Orange Bowl, and thanks to Andy Roddick beating Julien Jeanpierre at a tournament in Mexico, Federer rang in 1999 as the top-ranked junior player in the world (32).

To prepare for the rigors of the ATP Tour, Carter had to work on Federer's mindset and keep him patient. The perfectionist tendencies were still there, but Carter had harnessed them positively. Federer was still prone to the occasional on-court outburst, but his all-around game had evolved to where there were no glaring weakness an opponent could exploit.

Federer's first year on tour had everything one would expect from a rookie season, some stunning wins, some hard-to-fathom losses, and many takeaway lessons. The biggest one may have come at Wimbledon, where he squandered a two set to one lead and frittered away eight break points in the decisive fifth set of a first-round loss to Jiri Novak (33).

He played far better indoors than outdoors at first, losing nine straight outdoor matches when including his two Davis Cup defeats to Belgium. Federer failed to qualify for the main draw of the U.S. Open but later cracked the top 100 rankings by reaching the semifinals in Vienna. He capped the year with a challenger tournament victory in France and ended 1999 as the 64th-ranked player in the world (34).

The $223,859 in prize money certainly looked good to the 18-year-old Federer as well (35).

Federer's play continued to improve in 2000, highlighted by his first ATP Tour final appearance in Marseille and a third-round showing at the Australian Open that included a victory over Michael Chang (36). He also parted ways with Carter as a coach that spring and replaced him with Lundgren.

Federer viewed replacing Carter with the Swede as a natural progression in his career, and it made sense given that Lundgren had plenty of playing experience at all levels and also had faced some of the opponents Federer would be playing as a full-time player on the ATP Tour. Once a top 25 player on the tour, Lundgren could list victories over Agassi, Chang, Ivan Lendl, and Pat Cash to his credit, but the Swede's biggest asset would be the sharing the on-court mistakes he made with Federer (37).

Lundgren also had a stubborn streak that could match Federer's. He also had some prior experience dealing with such players, having coached Marcelo Rios for eight months in 1996. Lundgren helped the Chilean early in his career, and the mercurial Rios became the first South American player to reach number 1 in the world in 1998 (38).

The bonds of coach and player were tested quickly during the spring and summer as Federer endured a losing streak that featured first-round exits in Monte Carlo, Barcelona, Rome,

Hamburg, and St. Poelten (39). But in the unlikeliest of places, his fortunes turned at Roland Garros.

Federer ground his way into the fourth round of the French Open before losing to number 10 seed Alex Corretja in straight sets (40). But after a quarterfinal showing in Halle, he went into another funk, losing six consecutive first-round matches.

A tough third-round loss to 12th-seeded Juan Carlos Ferrero at the U.S. Open (41) provided a springboard that led to a fourth-place finish at the Olympics in Sydney (42). However, the disappointment of not claiming a medal Down Under was eased by the friendship and beginnings of a courtship with Mirka Vavrinec, a player on the Swiss women's tennis team who would later become the love of Federer's life (43).

It took until 2001 for Federer to claim his first ATP Tour title, and that happened at an indoor tournament in Milan. And he posted three three-set victories among his five matches, including in the finals against Julien Boutter (44).

Federer nearly added a second title in Rotterdam but lost to Nicolas Escude in the finals (45). By this point, he had cracked the top 20 in the world and made a strong run to the French Open quarterfinals where Corretja again dashed his hopes at Roland Garros (46).

His next big breakthrough came at Wimbledon that summer. Federer was seeded 15th at the all-England club and advanced to the fourth round to face four-time defending champion Pete Sampras, who was seeking his eighth title there.

Sampras carried a 31-match winning streak at Wimbledon into the match and had won 56 of his previous 57 contests there, but that legacy failed to unnerve the 19-year-old Federer in his Centre Court debut (47). The two engaged in a titanic match of blistering serves and crisp volleys.

Federer erased a set point in the first-set tiebreak, only to see Sampras regain his composure to win the second set. It was Federer's turn to respond, and he did, winning the third set with an emphatic ace on the line at set point. Sampras, showing all the attributes of a seven-time Wimbledon winner, held nothing back and ripped through a fourth-set tiebreak to set up a decisive fifth set.

The match delicately hung in the balance until the ninth game when Sampras earned two break points for a chance to go up 5-4 and serve for the match. Federer, though, played a volley at the net to erase the first and a well-placed forehand to nix the second and keep the match on serve.

In the 12th game, it was Federer who had two break points, but this time they were also match points. He only used the first, cracking back Sampras' serve for a winner and an end to the 7-6 (7), 5-7, 6-4, 6-7 (2), 7-5 contest (48).

The win marked a passing of the torch, though only symbolically as it would take Federer two more years to win his first Grand Slam title. He would lose to Tim Henman in five sets in the quarterfinals (49). The mental fatigue of the two biggest matches of his life as well as the strength-sapping physical demands of consecutive five-set contests were too much to overcome.

Sampras, though, would never win that elusive eighth title at the all-England club and added only one more Grand Slam victory after that defeat, his 2002 U.S. Open title.

Federer reached the fourth round of the U.S. Open in 2001, losing to Agassi in straight sets (50). While 2002 brought success in the form of titles in Sydney, Hamburg, and Vienna, it also delivered a devastating blow to Federer personally (51).

Carter, at only 37 years old, died in a tragic car accident in South Africa on August 1 of that year. Federer suggested South Africa as a newlywed vacation spot to Carter, which added to his grief and guilt to the point that he cried in the streets of Toronto the night before his defeat to Guillermo Canas (52).

"Thanks to him I have my entire technique and coolness," Federer recounted in an interview with The Australian. "He wasn't my first coach, but he was my real coach. He knew me and my game, and he always knew what was good for me." (53)

Over the final two months of the year, Federer played well enough to finish 2002 as the sixth-ranked player in the world. Grand Slam success eluded him in Melbourne and Roland Garros to start 2003 as he lost in the fourth and first rounds, respectively, but he also won titles in Marseille, Dubai, and Munich (54).

Chapter 3: First Major Title 2003
Wimbledon

Before his arrival at the all-England club, Federer tuned up for Wimbledon by playing the Gerry Weber Open in Germany. As the top seed, he won the title by dropping just one set in his five victories, capped by a 6-1, 6-3 triumph over Nicolas Kiefer (55).

But what was equally important was what came after his eighth career ATP Tour title – a week off. Lundgren arranged for Federer to arrive in England a week before the start of Wimbledon, changing things up from the previous year in which he lost in the first round.

Federer was the fourth seed, which put him in the top half of the draw and created a path for a potential semifinal matchup with defending champion and number 1 seed Hewitt. The Australian had the upper hand in the rivalry at this point, having won six of the eight lifetime head-to-head meetings (56).

Hewitt, though, wilted under a barrage of 19 aces by 6-foot-11 Ivo Karlovic, and the Croatian sprung a first-round upset in four sets that threw the tournament up for grabs from day one (57). Federer made sure there would not be a first-round exit of his own for the second straight year, dispatching Hyung-Taik Lee in straight sets in under two hours (58).

Federer was more efficient in the second round, blowing by Stefan Koubek in 77 minutes. His return game was on point, breaking the Austrian seven times while conceding just one game on serve (59).

The third round brought a challenge from promising American Mardy Fish, who had defeated 29th seed Gaston Gaudio in the first round. Federer dropped his first set of the tournament as Fish extended the match to a fourth set, but the Swiss star quickly ended any hopes of a rally with a 6-1 set to reach the round of 16 (60).

The two seeded players in the bottom half of Federer's group of 16 – number 16 Mikhail Youzhny and number 23 Agustin Calleri – were both bounced in the second round. Feliciano Lopez, who ousted Youzhny in straight sets, then did likewise with Flavio Saretta to face Federer (61).

The Spaniard was efficient with 13 aces, but despite playing with a bad back, Federer consistently pounced on Lopez's second serve and earned 18 break points. It was a very tight match, but Federer moved on with a narrow straight-set victory of 7-6 (7-5), 6-4, 6-4 (62).

For the second time in three years, Federer was in the Wimbledon quarterfinals. This time, his opponent was Dutchman and eighth-seeded Sjeng Schalken. Federer had won all three of the previous meetings between the two in 2003 without dropping a set, and that trend continued.

Federer's serve was on form as he cracked 13 aces to Schalken's one, and he won 50 of 62 points on his first serve. In just 98 minutes, Federer sent Schalken packing by a 6-3, 6-4, 6-4 score line to earn a date opposite fifth seed Roddick in his first Wimbledon and Grand Slam semifinal (63).

While Federer amassed a 21-3 lifetime record against Roddick (64), few pushed him as hard as the American, whose career total of one Grand Slam title can be partly attributed to having played in the same era as Federer and Rafael Nadal. This would be the first of four clashes between Federer and Roddick at the all-England club, and all four would end with Federer winning.

This contest, though, was about Federer staking a spot to being the world's best player. He played a stunningly brilliant game, turning Roddick's biggest weapon - a booming serve that could reach 140 miles per hour – against him with stinging returns. Federer also showcased his own strong service game, uncorking 17 aces, to further fluster the American.

The match swung in the first-set tiebreak with Roddick failing to convert a set point at 6-5 before Federer took the next three points. The Swiss star quickly held serve to start the second set and broke Roddick to go up 2-0. Federer's serve was just too good for Roddick to make any headway, and he faced only two break points in the entire match.

It was only fitting that Federer won the match by breaking the big-serving Roddick, converting a third match point when the American pushed a forehand wide (65). The event also showed Federer's serve and volley mastery as he dropped just 17 points in 15 games on serve (66).

As Federer tore through the top half of the 128-strong field, the bottom half descended into chaos. Mark Philippoussis rallied to stun number 2 seed Agassi in five sets in the fourth round on the strength of a Wimbledon record-tying 46 aces. Number 3 seed Ferrero also departed in round 16 (67).

By the time the dust settled, Philippoussis had made his way to his second career Grand Slam final, showing the serve-and-volley form from his run to the 1998 U.S. Open final that had escaped him in years past due to multiple knee surgeries.

This was the fourth meeting between the two, though Philippoussis was victorious in the most recent meeting in

Hamburg on clay. Federer won a singles match in the 2000 Davis Cup for Switzerland and a round of 32 matches the following year in Miami (68).

Both players quickly established their service games as the points came fast and furious. The adrenaline of a Grand Slam final produced thunderous serves, and they combined for 13 aces and zero break point chances to reach the first-set tiebreaker.

There, Philippoussis quickly gained a mini-break when Federer hit a backhand wide on the first point, but the Australian promptly gave it back when his drop shot floated wide. The two remained on serve until Philippoussis double-faulted for the third time in the set, giving Federer a mini-break at 6-4 and two set points. The Aussie saved the first one on his serve but sent a service return wide on the next one to give Federer the first set 7-6.

Riding that momentum, Federer took control of the match at the start of the second set. After Philippoussis had unloaded his seventh ace to make it 15-all, Federer laced two successive forehand winners, including one cross court as he displayed remarkable baseline speed to blunt Philippoussis' serve-and-volley tactics.

He converted his first break point when Philippoussis dumped a backhand into the net and quickly consolidated the break with three aces in his next service game to go up 2-0. Federer then used his one-handed backhand to devastating effect on the Aussie's next service game, breaking him again, and by the time the Swiss star delivered his 14th ace of the match on set point, he was one set from his first Grand Slam title.

Federer's numbers through the first two sets were unfathomable. He had committed just three unforced errors while smacking 34 winners to go with those 14 aces. Philippoussis was not playing all that poorly; this was Federer simply carrying his elite level of play from his semifinal victory into the final.

Philippoussis got to deuce for the first time on Federer's serve in the fourth game of the third set, but he never earned a break point as Federer hit a forehand winner and another ace to slam the door shut and even the set 2-2. The two remained on serve for the rest of the set and went to a second tiebreak.

Federer grabbed a mini-break on the first point of the tiebreaker but lost it with a rare error before staying on serve to make it 2-1. It truly was Federer's day because, on the next point, he mishit a forehand return of Philippoussis' 130-mile-per-hour serve, but it looped over the charging Aussie and comfortably in to restore the mini-break.

That became a full break when Philippoussis hit a long backhand while at the net, and Federer then charged ahead 6-1 with an ace and unforced error by Philippoussis. The Aussie summoned some professional pride to hold serve and stave off two championship points, but Federer was not going to be denied.

Philippoussis dumped a backhand into the net, and Federer sunk to his knees to celebrate his first Grand Slam title. He was briefly overcome with emotion as he sat to absorb the atmosphere before saluting the crowd.

Federer became just the fourth player to win both the Wimbledon junior singles and gentlemen's singles titles in the Open Era, joining all-time great Bjorn Borg, Pat Cash, and his idol Stefan Edberg. Near the end of the NBC telecast, analyst John McEnroe noted that Federer would be in line for "many, many more majors, not just Wimbledon" (69).

Few realized how prescient his words would prove to be.

Chapter 4: Rise to Number 1 and Dominance

Federer won only two more titles in 2003, successfully defending his trophy in Vienna and the ATP's season-ending event in Houston in which he steamrolled Roddick and Agassi in the semifinals and finals. He had reached number 2 in the rankings by year's end and was hot on Roddick's heels for the number 1 spot (70).

Federer opened 2004 at the Australian Open as the number 2 seed. He did not run into any difficulties until the fourth round when Hewitt had an entire continent on his side and took the first set. Federer, though, buckled down to drop only seven games the rest of the match to advance. By the time Federer reached the final opposite Marat Safin, who had vanquished both Agassi and Roddick, the world's top spot was there for the taking (71).

The final also marked the unofficial end of the Sampras-Agassi reign, though no one had projected Federer to be the one who would pull away from a group of peers that included Safin, Hewitt, and Nalbandian, among others. But it was here in Melbourne where that separation began.

Safin had little left in the tank by the time he got to the finals, and his cumulative playing time in his six victories was eight hours more than Federer's. After the Swiss star had won the first-set tiebreaker, there was not much resistance left for Safin, and the straight-set win gave Federer his second Grand Slam title in his last three appearances (72).

After wins in Dubai, Indian Wells, and Hamburg before the French Open, Federer was done in at Roland Garros by the only foreign tennis player perhaps as loved as Nadal in France. Three-time champion and Brazilian Gustavo Kuerten played a near-flawless game and sent the Swiss star packing in straight sets in the third round.

Federer traded breaks with Kuerten in the first two games of the match, but could not find any rhythm against the Brazilian and failed to even find a break point against Kuerten the remainder of the match (73).

He quickly regrouped to defend his title in Halle and produced a clinical defense of his Wimbledon title. He dropped just one set in his first six wins in his march back to the final, where this time he would face Roddick. The American was eager to add a second Grand Slam title to his collection after winning the U.S. Open the previous year (74).

That eagerness showed as Roddick came out smashing Federer's return with full gusto in winning the first set. Federer was fortunate to survive a charge by Roddick in the second set, taking full advantage of a net cord to win the set point with a thunderous forehand.

A rain delay in the third set with Roddick up 2-1 and a break stunted the American's momentum as Federer came out of the delay to bring the match back to serve. The Swiss star used a pair of his trademark backhands to grab the tiebreaker 7-3 and a one-set advantage.

Federer fought off a staggering six break points to deny Roddick an early advantage and broke him at love to gain a 4-3 lead. Once more, Federer sunk to his knees after winning on match point, and there were tears of joy for a second straight year at Centre Court of the all-England club (75).

After a surprising second-round exit in the Olympics at the hands of Tomas Berdych (76), Federer and Vavrinec arrived a week early in New York. The two caught a pair of Broadway shows ahead of the tournament, but the spotlight shone brightest on Federer in that fortnight (77).

His quarterfinal match against Agassi stretched into two days because of rain, and the windy conditions when they resumed nearly did in Federer as Agassi forced a fifth set. But a net cord gave Federer a crucial break to go up 5-3, and he closed out the match on serve to advance (78).

He disposed of Henman in the semifinals and then put together one of the greatest performances of his career in a Grand Slam final by overwhelming Hewitt 6-0, 7-6 (3), 6-0 for his first U.S. Open title and fourth Slam victory of his career.

Federer became the first person to win three majors in a year since Mats Wilander in 1988, and the first to go 4-0 in his first four Grand Slam finals. He beat Hewitt at various points in all three of his Grand Slam victories that year, so it was no surprise that the Australian felt it was possible Federer could reach Sampras' seemingly unassailable mark of 14 Grand Slam titles (79).

He wrapped up a banner 2004 with titles in Bangkok and Houston, going 11-0 in finals in the calendar year. Federer finished with a 74-6 record and more than $6.3 million in prize money (80).

Federer was a virtuoso soloist in 2004, but in 2005, a rival emerged to challenge his supremacy. He was unable to defend his title in Melbourne, losing in a five-set thriller to Safin in the semifinals. Safin's run to the finals that year included a first-round demolition of Djokovic, who was making his Grand Slam debut (76).

It was also the last time there would be a Grand Slam final without Federer, Nadal, or Djokovic until the 2014 U.S. Open, a span of 38 Grand Slam events.

Any disappointments of being denied a fifth Grand Slam title were not apparent as Federer racked up titles in Rotterdam, Dubai, Indian Wells, and Miami. In the finals of the Ericsson Open, he rallied from two sets down to defeat the 29th-seeded Nadal, avenging a loss to the Spaniard the previous year there in the round of 32 (81).

At the French Open, the 19-year-old Nadal gained a measure of revenge with a four-set win over Federer in the semifinals. One could begin to see the parallels in the career arcs of these two rivals, with the young Spaniard hungry to close out the world's top-ranked player as darkness descended at Roland Garros (82).

Nadal would become the first player to win the French Open in his Roland Garros debut since Wilander in 1982, and that title marked the beginning of an era of dominance on the red clay that will likely never be equaled (83).

Back on his favorite surface, though, Federer again proved to be peerless on the grass at Wimbledon. He needed to rally from two sets down to defeat Nicolas Kiefer in the third round and bested Hewitt in the semis before facing Roddick in the final for the second straight year.

This time, however, Federer was in no mood for charity. He shredded Roddick in straight sets, winning his third consecutive Wimbledon title in a mere 101 minutes (84). The American felt he played a better game than in last year's final, but he also elegantly conceded that Federer "played head and shoulders above what he played last year."

That momentum carried into the hardcourt season in the United States with a win at the Cincinnati Masters and a successful title defense in the U.S. Open for his sixth Grand Slam title. Once more, he vanquished Hewitt in the semifinals of a slam and this time ran into the 35-year-old Agassi, making his 20th U.S. Open appearance.

The match had all the hallmarks of the changing of the guard in the sport, though Agassi refused to yield graciously and was backed by the always-vociferous New York crowd. Federer won the first set, but Agassi turned back the clock with a vintage performance in the second, stalking Federer's suddenly weak backhand and counterpunching the Swiss star's serve to even the match.

That momentum carried into the third set where Federer found himself trailing 2-4. But the Swiss star leveled the match and kept it on serve until the tiebreaker. Agassi won the first point with an exquisitely placed drop shot, but Federer regained his bearings and ripped off the next seven points of the tiebreaker to break Agassi's will.

And to leave no doubt, he won the first five games of the fourth set before Agassi staved off two championship points on serve. Federer, though, quickly closed out the contest for his sixth Grand Slam title, bringing him level with boyhood idols Becker and Stefan Edberg (85).

Though a loss to Nalbandian in the season-ending ATP Tour final denied him the 12th title in 2005, Federer finished with a gaudy 81-4 record that year and another season of more than $6 million in prize money (86).

Federer started 2006 right where he left off: winning. His first appearance in Doha resulted in a title, and that led to a seventh Grand Slam title and second Australian Open crown. Federer, though, had to work in this tournament as he dropped sets in each of the last four matches.

He fell behind to Marcos Baghdatis 5-7, 0-2 before winning the contest in four sets against the unseeded Cypriot in the final (87). But this was the first time the Federer publicly acknowledged the challenge of trying to chase Sampras. The 24-year-old met Rod Laver for the first time, and by this point in the Australian's career, he had already won the calendar Grand Slam.

Laver turned professional that year, and as a result missed out on participating in a total of 24 Grand Slam events from 1963-68. Any doubts about Laver's standing among the greats in the sport despite finishing with "only" 11 Grand Slam titles are quickly erased when you realize he repeated the calendar Grand Slam in 1969 and remains the last men's player to accomplish the feat (88).

The gaping hole that was the lack of a French Open title had already begun to gnaw at Federer, who was now crafting his schedule to peak for the four slams. Nadal, though, was now a holy terror on clay. He beat Federer in the finals at both Monte Carlo and Rome, gaining the psychological upper hand ahead of Roland Garros following a draining five-set match that took nearly five hours in Italy (89).

But everyone not named Rafael Nadal offered little resistance to Federer in Paris. He dropped one set in the six victories, which was one less than the Spaniard did in returning to defend his title. Federer, though, had the chance to complete the "Roger Slam," and held all four titles simultaneously.

And it started out perfectly for Federer, who won the first five games of the match and quickly took the first set. But it turned out to be fool's gold for Federer, who uncharacteristically fell apart in the second after Nadal broke him to go up 2-0. He committed 16 unforced errors as Nadal evened the match and then squandered three break points up 2-1 in the third.

Nadal followed with a crushing break to go up 3-2 and served out to win that set. In the fourth, the Spaniard took control of the tiebreak with four straight points and laced a forehand winner to seal the match and a successful defense of his French Open title (90).

Federer, though, would regroup once more at Wimbledon where he would claim his fourth successive title. He also made history by eclipsing Bjorn Borg's 41-game winning streak on grass with his first-round win over Richard Gasquet (91).

But this was also the tournament where Nadal proved he would not be an easy out on any surface anymore. The Spaniard had surprisingly reached the final despite being the number 2 seed and gained some credibility by rallying from two sets down in the second round and easing past Agassi in the third.

The ground and pound of the baseline Nadal so often enjoyed in Paris were now mixed with the grace and speed outside London by a player who never conceded that any shot was out of reach anywhere on the court.

The first set was the same story as Paris, but with a different style as Federer drove Nadal mad with sliced backhands to win the first set in 25 minutes. But Federer left the door open in the second set with a balky serve, and Nadal finally found a groove.

Here, though, was where the experience of Federer in his 36th match on grass and Nadal's 12th showed. It was Nadal who went haywire with his forehand serving for the set and again on two occasions during the tiebreaker as Federer escaped with a two sets to none advantage.

The third set, though, provided ample evidence that Nadal was going to win a title at Wimbledon regardless of the opponent. Time and again, he would get to a well-placed Federer shot and return it with malice and precision. Nadal took the third-set tiebreaker, which was also the only set Federer dropped that fortnight, to extend the match.

Federer responded to the urgency of the situation as a champion would, breaking Nadal twice to take a commanding 5-1 lead. Nadal had one last gasp with a break and held to draw within 5-3, but Federer served out the match to join Borg and Sampras as the only players to win four straight Wimbledon titles in the Open era (92).

For the second consecutive season, Federer would claim three Grand Slam titles in a calendar year as he successfully defended his U.S. Open title. Similar to Wimbledon, Federer tore through his opponents and did not drop a set en route to the final.

There once more was Roddick, the 2003 champ who was looking to prevent Federer from a third straight title in New York. For a while the two were on equal terms; they split the first two sets and had combined to fight off nine break points in successive games in the third.

But in trying to force a third-set tiebreaker, Roddick broke down. A vintage sizzling Federer backhand put him down 0-30, and Roddick never recovered as Federer took the set, and eventually, the match. He was now at nine Grand Slam titles and finished the four majors that year with a 27-1 mark, with only Nadal standing between him and tennis immortality (93).

Federer closed 2006 on a 29-match winning streak as he ended the year with a staggering 92-5 record. Only two players beat him that year: Nadal and Murray (94).

Grand Slam title number 10 came in Melbourne in impressive fashion. Federer did not drop a set the entire tournament and was pushed to a tiebreak only three times. He bounced Djokovic in the fourth round and outclassed Roddick in the semis (95).

Federer did have to save two set points in the first set of the final against Fernando Gonzalez, who torched Nadal in straight sets in the semis, but he quickly regrouped and became the first player to win a major without dropping a set since Borg at the 1980 French Open. Federer also equaled Jack Crawford's 73-year standard of reaching the final in seven consecutive majors (96).

The win also ensured he would surpass Jimmy Connors' record of being atop the ATP rankings for 160 consecutive weeks when March rolled around (97).

Federer's 41-match win streak came to an end with a first-round loss to Guillermo Canas at Indian Wells (98), but an important title came in Hamburg. He rallied to defeat Nadal in three sets to end the Spaniard's incredible 81-match win streak on clay (99).

That boost of confidence served Federer well at Roland Garros as he made his way back to the final for a second straight year. And yet again, here was Nadal hell-bent on preventing a "Roger Slam" to claim a third consecutive French Open title for himself.

And as was the case in the previous year's French Open, Federer started brightly. He put Nadal on his heels at times, but could never put him away. The plucky Spaniard fought off ten break points in an opening set that demoralized Federer.

Nadal's dominance on the clay is as pronounced as Federer's on grass. Though Federer won the second set (the only one Nadal dropped in the fortnight), there was never a point when Nadal failed to control this match. Federer's usually reliable forehand was anything but as he committed a whopping 29 unforced errors on that side and 59 overall (100).

The disappointment sat with Federer long enough that he bypassed his usual Wimbledon warm-up in Germany and went straight to the all-England club for his next tournament. Everything fell into place as Federer cruised into the final, and even played one less match since Haas could not play in the fourth round due to injury (101).

But there again, in the final, awaited Nadal. By this point, Federer had been number 1 for 178 consecutive weeks, and

Nadal had been number 2 for the last 101 of them. There was barely any margin between the players save the dominance on their respective surfaces of choice, and even that was eroding to Nadal's favor.

But it was still not the Spaniard's time at the all-England club, though not out of lack of effort and desire. Nadal ground his way through two five-set matches among his six victories and logged nearly 15 hours of tennis compared to Federer's 9:03 in his five.

The two were entrenched in their long-successful ways, with Federer's serve in imperious form and Nadal content to use his speed on the baseline to rip returns with either hand. The first set was a stalemate, won by Federer in a tiebreak. Nadal leveled things in the second, and the tense slugfest carried into the third.

Federer's serve, though, was wearing on Nadal, and his 16th ace of the match provided a 4-2 tiebreak advantage that proved too much for the Spaniard to overcome. Nadal, though, responded with some blistering baseline play to break Federer twice and force a decisive fifth set.

And much like the French Open where Nadal wobbled but did not fall, here did Federer. He fought off two break points in both the first and third games of the set to stay on serve and then broke Nadal emphatically in the sixth game with three consecutive forehand winners to go up 4-2.

Another break to close the match gave Federer his 11th Grand Slam title and his fifth in a row at Wimbledon, putting him in the rarified air of Borg for consecutive titles won there (102). No longer was it a question of if Federer would catch Sampras, but where and when? For Nadal, it was no longer a question of if he would win at Wimbledon, but when (103)?

The U.S. Open that year tested all of Federer's resolve. He had to navigate a challenging path, beating fifth-seeded Roddick in the quarterfinals and number 4 seed Nikolai Davydenko in the semis (104). But in the final, a new opponent was set to prevent Federer from winning Grand Slam title number 12.

Djokovic had steadily climbed the ranks of the ATP Tour since his Grand Slam debut at the 2005 Australian Open and was making his first finals appearance at a major. The Serbian had a similar all-around game to Federer but was also a work in progress. He also had a headstrong temperament similar to Federer that fostered a reputation of petulance.

Federer exploited that lack of experience on the big stage as he fought off seven set points from Djokovic, including five in the first set when down 5-6 and love-40. The two set points Federer saved while on serve in the second set broke the young Serbian's will as he cracked an ace and watched a Djokovic backhand sail long.

The 20-year-old Djokovic looked nothing like the Djokovic who rose to number 1 in this current decade. Here he was unsteady and unable to take advantage of Federer, who was having an off day by his lofty standards but still producing enough quality play to make sure Djokovic never found any rhythm.

Even after closing out the match by Djokovic netting a backhander, Federer conceded the straight-set victory was, "a bit brutal for Novak, to be honest." But Federer also knew a future rivalry was building, and the stranglehold he and Nadal shared at the summit of men's singles was going to be contested (105).

That breakthrough for Djokovic came quickly as he stunned Federer in straight sets in the semifinals of the Australian Open in 2008, ending his run of consecutive Grand Slam finals appearances at 10 (106). The Serb would defeat Jo-Wilfried Tsonga in the finals for his first Grand Slam title, cementing his status as the world's number 3 player and giving both Federer and Nadal something to think about going forward.

Federer's build-up for the French Open was uneven, losing to Nadal in the finals in Monte Carlo and Hamburg around a quarterfinal loss in Rome to Radek Stepanek. There was still a gulf in talent large enough for Federer to make a third straight finals appearance at Roland Garros (107).

This time, however, Nadal was in the best form of his life. Whether it was the anger of being slighted as the number 2 seed despite his 21-0 record in Paris entering the tournament, or whatever the reason, Nadal's on-court rage was as red as the clay he stalked around on.

And for whatever reason, Federer just did not have it on this day. When those two factors combined, the resulting scoreline between the top two players in the world forced a double-take it was so unlikely.

6-1, 6-3, 6-0.

Federer finished with 35 unforced errors to Nadal's seven. Nadal had at least one break point in all but one of Federer's service games. In addition to the already lethal topspin forehand Nadal possessed to create his dominance, he showed an all-around game of sliced backhands and some volleys, as if to show Federer what was to come to Wimbledon.

It was the worst defeat in any of the 173 Grand Slam matches Federer had played to that point in his career. It was the first time he failed to win a game in a set in any match since 1999. He felt so chastened by the loss which took place in 108 minutes that he apologized to the crowd post-match (108).

Federer found solace in his Wimbledon warm-up in Germany, rolling through Halle without dropping a game while on serve (109). There was comfort again at the all-England club as Federer rolled through his six matches in straight sets, disposing of Hewitt in the fourth round and a resurgent Safin in the semifinals.

On the bottom half of the draw, Nadal was doing his part of setting up a third straight finals appearance between the two at the all-England club. His biggest win of the six was a clinical rout of Murray in straight sets, and Nadal had dropped just one set before the final (110).

In these matches, it was usually Federer who started strong, but in this instance, Nadal took the offensive. He broke Federer early to take a 2-1 lead and fought off three break points in two different games, including at 5-4 to win the first set.

Nadal pressed the advantage further in the second set, overcoming a break by Federer with two of his own as part of a

48

five-game run that put him on the verge of a stunning straight-set victory at Wimbledon.

Federer, though, dug a line. While he could not get through to break Nadal, he finally found his service game to keep the Spaniard at bay. The two held serve until a rain delay at 5-4 with Federer ahead halted play for a half-hour. Though the rain relented, the deluge of Federer aces continued, and he capped off the third-set tiebreaker with one to extend the match.

The fourth set is one of lore that puts this game among the best played in the sport. Again, the two titans held serve throughout the set, resulting in another tiebreaker. Federer grabbed a mini-break with a forehand winner after Nadal made an athletic backhand stab of a shot at the net.

Nadal, though, quickly grabbed it back with a net point and then went ahead 2-1 when Federer pushed a forehand wide. An ace wide made it 3-1, and a serve that hit the line prevented any good return as Nadal pushed his advantage to 4-1.

Federer finally stopped the bleeding with a forehand winner, but he sailed a backhand wide to give Nadal a 5-2 lead and a chance to serve out the match for the title. But the Spaniard double-faulted, giving Federer some life. Then the momentum swung Federer's way as Nadal netted a backhand to make it 5-4.

It was a lifeline, yes, but Federer was still in grave danger. His serve forced Nadal wide, and Federer crushed the service return with a forehand to the opposite corner that even Nadal could not chase down. A service winner gave Federer a 6-5 lead and set point.

Now it was Nadal's turn to counterpunch, and a lengthy rally ended with Federer slapping a forehand wide. A second changeover took place with Nadal still on serve, and after Federer had hit a forehand long, Nadal earned his first championship point up 7-6.

Federer stood tall once more, getting a service winner which was upheld by video review. Nadal answered with a haymaker of his own, ripping a two-handed passing shot on the run by a charging Federer. Another championship point earned.

Nadal pushed Federer wide with his service, and it gave the Spaniard time to come around behind the backhand return to charge the net. Nadal hit a forehand to pin Federer, but he smoked a backhand to stave off the second match point and knot tie tiebreaker at 8.

Federer ran Nadal ragged on the next point before putting it away with a forehand, and he forced the decisive fifth set as a backhand by Nadal sailed inches long (111). The fifth set featured another half-hour rain delay at 2-2, but the two players battled each other and the impending darkness, unable to crack the other's serve.

With no tiebreaker to decide the title, the two players stayed on serve for the first 14 games of the set, with Nadal finding small cracks in Federer's armor. But on the third break point at 7-7, Federer sent a forehand long, giving Nadal a break and another opportunity at the title.

Not that Federer would abandon his crown easily. Down 30-40, Federer fended off a third championship point with a backhand winner. But Nadal would quickly earn a fourth, and this time, a netted forehand by Federer ended his reign at the all-England club. A 13th Grand Slam title would have to wait, and the gap between numbers 1 and 2 became closer still (112).

Nadal formally ended Federer's reign as the number 1 player in the world following Federer's quarterfinal loss in the Olympics in Beijing, his run complete at 237 weeks (113). But if there was any disappointment from falling to number 2, it did not show as Federer rebounded to win the U.S. Open title by routing Murray. Like Djokovic the previous year, Murray was seeking his first Grand Slam title in his first major finals appearance.

This time, though, Federer put together a complete display in winning his fifth consecutive U.S. Open title, running through Murray in less than two hours. The spark and sizzle of his all-around game returned, overwhelming the young Scot and seizing control of the match by breaking Murray at love to end the second set 7-5.

Federer ensured that he would finish the year with at least one major title and move within one of Sampras' all-time mark. Where that would come, however, no one was sure as the new pecking order of Nadal, Federer, Djokovic, and Murray was clearly being established (114).

Nadal's confidence rightfully soared heading into the new year, and he defeated Federer in another five-set final in Melbourne. This loss stung Federer because he knew he had squandered opportunities early in the match against the Spaniard.

Nadal was a tired player in this final, having needed five sets to eliminate Fernando Verdasco in the semifinals. Federer tried to press the advantage early and was up 4-2, but Nadal sprayed baseline winners to rally and take the first set.

The third set was even worse for Federer as he failed to capitalize on six break points and lost the tiebreak. This was due in part to a ridiculous backhand drop volley Nadal hit that provided a set point he would immediately convert.

This five-setter lacked the drama of last summer's Wimbledon, but in the end, it was another loss for Federer. He knew a chance to match Sampras had come and gone, his voice cracking as he said, "God, it's killing me," when he tried to address the crowd post-match (115).

Nadal, never a stranger to the emotions of the moment, put an arm around Federer in consolation, and that iconic image of the two in Melbourne embodied the state of men's singles in the 2000s (116).

Federer was winless in 2009 until defeating Nadal in the finals of the Madrid Masters, though he also took six weeks off to deal with back spasms. But there had been false dawns like this ahead of the French Open previously for the Swiss star. And now there was the baggage of losing three consecutive Grand Slam finals to Nadal around his U.S. Open title. What was it going to take to dethrone the world's number 1 ranked player on his most dominant surface?

Sometimes, though, fate intervenes. And this springtime in Paris, it came in the form of up-and-comer Robin Soderling. The 25-year-old was seeded 23rd in the French Open and had dropped one set in his three victories, though he did need tiebreakers in five sets over that span (117).

Still, no one gave him any chance against Nadal, who was 31-0 by this point at Roland Garros and steaming towards a fifth straight French Open title. Nadal, in fact, had dropped five games total in routing Hewitt to reach the fourth round opposite Soderling, who had never been this deep in a Grand Slam (118).

What made this upset even more surreal was that one month prior in Rome, Nadal had throttled Soderling, dropping just one game against him (119). Here, though, Soderling went for broke and came up aces with a consequences-be-damned aggressive approach.

And every time Nadal seemed to find an avenue back into the game, Soderling had an answer. By the time the fourth-set tiebreak came and went, it was Soderling who had done the unthinkable and dealt Nadal his first loss on the red clay of Roland Garros (120).

Soderling did not stop there. His feel-good adventure in the top half of the draw continued with upsets of the 10th-seeded Davydenko and number 12 Fernando Gonzalez in the next two rounds to reach the final (121). Federer, meanwhile, had to deal with the increased scrutiny that came with his chase of a

Sampras-equaling 14th major that would also complete a career Grand Slam without the pressure of facing Nadal.

That road, though, was anything but easy. Federer nearly joined Nadal on the sidelines in the fourth round, rallying from two sets down and a break point at 3-4 in the third set to defeat Haas. The match swung when Federer saved that break point with a thunderous inside-out forehand that left Haas flat-footed.

Federer held serve, broke Haas the following game, and dropped just two games the rest of the match (122). He eased past Gael Monfils in the quarters before surviving another five-set tussle, this time against Martin del Potro (123).

The only drama in the final against Soderling, though, came from a fan who rushed onto the court in the second set and tried to put a hat on Federer before being tackled by a security guard. Before that unscheduled interruption, Federer was dominant. He rolled through the first set in 26 minutes and shook off the anxiety created by the fan by taking the second in a tiebreak.

Serving for the match at 5-4 in the third set was almost too much for Federer, who said afterward, "it was almost unplayable for me." He served out the match, once more dropping to his knees in tears to celebrate a Grand Slam title, but doing so on the red clay of Roland Garros for the first time.

His emotions got the better of him throughout the post-match ceremony, crying through the playing of the Swiss national anthem and upon receiving the trophy from Agassi. That carried particular weight as he joined the American as one of six players to complete the career Grand Slam, an accomplishment Sampras did not achieve as he amassed his 14 titles.

The burden finally removed from his shoulders, Federer probably understated the feeling post-match when he said, "Now, for the rest of my career, I can play relaxed and never hear again that I never won the French Open," (124).

Finally level with Sampras, Federer's first opportunity to move into sole possession of the all-time mark came at his favorite hunting grounds, Wimbledon. There would be no potential rematch of the riveting final from last year since Nadal was forced to withdraw shortly before the start of the tournament due to tendinitis in his knees, leaving Federer as the de facto top seed (125).

He played the role to the hilt, dropping just one set en route to the final, but working harder to get there as he played five tiebreakers. Soderling got a second crack at Federer in the round of 16 and played better, but he still could not take a set off

Federer in a tight straight-set defeat that featured two of those tiebreakers (126).

While Nadal never made the trip to England, Djokovic was bounced in the quarterfinals by Haas (127), and the burden that Murray had to endure as England's next great hope to win Wimbledon was too much to bear with a semifinal loss to Roddick (128).

This was the fourth time the two would meet in a Grand Slam final, and the third time it took place at Wimbledon. And the two put on a match as good as the year before, with a fifth set for the ages.

As history beckoned, the greats of both the locale and the sport were in attendance: Laver, Borg, and Sampras. The who's who of tennis at Wimbledon and all-time were on hand and treated to a throwback at the all-England club.

It was classic Wimbledon: thunderous serves followed up with charges to the net for quick points on half-volleys. Roddick was enjoying a renaissance season despite being ranked sixth in the world, the gulf in class between himself and the top four on a week-to-week basis may as well been the English Channel before he strung together his six victories.

As was the case in 2004, it was Roddick on the front foot as he took the first set. But what could have been for the American in the second will gnaw at him until his final days. Roddick had four set points in the tiebreak and failed to cash in any of them as Federer rallied to win six straight points.

The most glaring of these mishits came at set point at 6-5, when Roddick mistimed a volley with the whole court begging. But unlike finals past, the Yank did not wilt when faced with adversity. Federer fought him off in a third set tiebreak only to have Roddick respond with his best tennis in the fourth set to force a winner-take-all fifth.

And what a fifth set it was. It was what the British call "blood and thunder" when they describe soccer, a test of physical fortitude that manifested itself here in the form of holding serve in a battle of nerves. By this point, Federer's service game was imperious. He cracked three aces in the fourth game, two in the sixth, and three more in the eighth.

Roddick was not piling up aces at such a staggering rate, but Federer had all sorts of trouble handling a first serve that topped out at 145 miles per hour. At 4-5, Federer put only one ball in play on Roddick's serve. In turn, the few serves Roddick was able to put in play did not manifest themselves into any points of importance until the 16th game.

There, Roddick earned himself two break points, only to have Federer scramble them away with a serve and volley and a forehand winner. Federer then won the next two points to keep the match on serve at 8-8.

The tense battle continued with no quarter given. The fifth set reached the hour mark in the 20th game. Federer got to deuce at 11-10, only to have Roddick pump two serves down the middle that resulted in easy points to extend the match. Roddick took a 15-30 lead in the 24th game, but Federer responded by unleashing three consecutive aces.

The Swiss star finally was starting to find some places to exploit Roddick's serve, pushing the 25th game to deuce and nicking two more in game 27. Federer's career-high 50th and final ace of the match provided a 30-love lead as he held serve at love to make it 15-14.

Those extended points on Roddick's serve finally paid off in the 30th game. Two unforced errors gave Federer a love-30 lead, but Roddick ripped off three straight points. Another unforced error brought the game back to deuce, but Roddick had a game point following a service winner.

Federer was the beneficiary of another unforced error, then gained his only championship point after another Roddick backhand sailed long. On match point, Roddick pulled a forehand wide to end a short rally, and a back-and-forth clash that lasted 4 hours and 17 minutes finally had its victor.

It was the only break of Roddick's serve in 38 games. It turned out to be the only one Federer needed (129).

It was Federer who stood alone as the sport's winningest player in Grand Slam men's singles titles, and he also reclaimed the number 1 ranking from Nadal. He passed Sampras with number 15, and the former great ceded his place gracefully to the Swiss star after the match, saying, "He could get 17, 18 majors when it's all done. He's a stud," (130).

His place in history now secure, Federer went about trying to create more distance between himself and Sampras to leave no doubt about the greatest player of all-time. It seemed like a fait accompli that Federer would become the first player since Bill Tilden to win six straight U.S. Open titles, but the unheralded Argentine del Potro would have other ideas.

It was one of the rare matches Federer lost his cool. The replay challenges del Potro made were both timely and correct. Down 4-5 in the second set, the Argentine made one such challenge on a forehand the line judge ruled out and got the point reversed. In the third set, Federer berated umpire Jake Garner over del Potro taking too long to challenge a call, even using an expletive to get his point across.

Federer's rare breakdown gave del Potro an avenue into the match, and he took full advantage. Using a blistering forehand, he was able to take a fourth-set tiebreak from Federer and then broke him early in the fifth for a 2-0 lead. The Argentine then broke him one last time to win the match and claimed his only Grand Slam title to date (131).

Despite failing to win any other tournaments in 2009, Federer ended the year as the world's top-ranked player. But more importantly, he had secured his place as arguably the top-ranked player in the sport (132).

He finally added that 16th slam in Melbourne, claiming his fourth Australian Open title. There was little drama as Federer dropped only one set the entire tournament, and again denied Murray his first Grand Slam title with a straight-set triumph.

The match swung with two breaks by Federer bridging the first two sets. The first gave him a 5-3 lead and allowed him to serve out the first set. The ensuing break to open the second set provided an advantage too large for Murray to overcome against Federer's dominant service game.

The Scot squandered plenty of chances to extend the match in a third-set tiebreak, losing five set points, but Federer also let two match points slip away. He would not waste the third one, winning the title when Murray dumped a backhand into the net (133).

By the time the French Open rolled around, Federer was in the unfamiliar position of defending champion at Roland Garros and was the top seed. That left Nadal number 2 and chomping at the bit to re-establish his dominance at the court he knew every square inch of. But that opportunity never presented itself because, again, fate presented itself in the form of Soderling.

The Swede had put together a solid campaign against everyone on the ATP Tour not named Roger Federer and entered Roland Garros as the fifth seed. Soderling was out to prove his run to last year's finals was no fluke, and he reached the quarterfinals in impressive fashion, dropping only one set (134).

Federer did him one better by winning all 12 of his sets and had every reason to believe his mastery of the Swede would continue. His three victories over Soderling in last year's Grand

Slam events was part of a spotless 12-0 lifetime record in their matchups (135).

Soderling, though, proved that 13 was a lucky number for him. He loaded up on his forehand against Federer, similar to the way he stunned Nadal the year before, and grabbed control of the match by breaking Federer for a 6-5 advantage in the third set. He added another one early in the fourth and was on his way for a return trip to the final, and an eventual loss to Nadal.

The swing in fortunes at Roland Garros cost Federer the number 1 spot in the world as Nadal regained the catbird's seat. It also ended Federer's record run of 23 straight Grand Slam semifinal appearances (136).

That streak of non-semifinal appearances would reach two at Wimbledon where Berdych pulled off a four-set stunner (137). The struggles continued in the semifinals of the U.S. Open where Federer let Djokovic escape twice on match point as the Serb rallied for a five-set victory (138).

Even winning the year-ending ATP Tour final in London did little to soothe Federer. As his chasing of Nadal for the number 1 ranking became more labored, so did his fight to hold off Djokovic for number 2 (139).

In 2011, Federer endured his first barren year without a Grand Slam title since 2002. He would lose to Djokovic in the semifinals of the Australian Open, but gained a small measure of revenge by ending the Serb's 41-match win streak to start the year with a victory in the French Open semifinals (140).

But a finals appearance at Roland Garros meant another date with Nadal. It was a high-quality tennis match, but for Federer, it ended the same way as all his other matches against the Spaniard on the red clay, with a defeat. But this loss began to raise questions about Federer's legacy. Nadal now had six French Open titles to his credit, had completed his own career Grand Slam the previous fall at the U.S. Open, and had now reached double figures in major titles (141).

While Federer had received all the accolades in passing Sampras to become the all-time leader in slam titles, people rightfully wondered if Nadal could overtake Federer. He was then ousted in the quarterfinals at Wimbledon, but it was his defeat to Djokovic in the semifinals of the U.S. Open for the second straight year that turned the whispers of Federer's decline in play to full-fledged open discussions.

In Federer's defense, though, the loss to Djokovic turned on a one-in-a-million shot that cemented the Serb's standing among the game's elite and propelled him into the talk of all-time greats. Up 5-3 and on serve in the fifth set, Federer had two match points, and for all intents and purposes, was in control of the match.

With absolutely nothing to lose facing Federer's serve, Djokovic seared a cross-court service return that stayed in and extended the game. Giddy at the moment, Djokovic turned to the crowd for the praise of such a magnificent shot, and they responded. Whether or not it unnerved Federer is uncertain, but it certainly sparked Djokovic (142).

The Serb staved off the second match point and broke Federer as part of a stunning five-game run to close the match with a 7-5 fifth-set victory. For a player so used to winning these important games and now coming to grips with a group of opponents who were getting the better of him on a more consistent basis, Djokovic's shot was just too much to bear in the heat of the moment after the loss.

"Confidence? Are you kidding me?" an exasperated Federer said post-match. "I mean, please. Some players grow up and play like that – being down 5-2 in the third, and they all just start slapping shots. I never played that way. I believe hard work's going to pay off, because early on, maybe I didn't always work my hardest.

"How can you play a shot like that on match point? Maybe he's been doing it for 20 years, so for him, it was very normal. You've got to ask him," (143).

The Grand Slam drought extended into 2012 with a pair of semifinal losses, first to Nadal in the Australian Open and then Djokovic in the French Open (144). By this point, it was now Djokovic who was in the ascendancy and the top-ranked player in the world, further adding to Federer's frustration. But like a pair of comfortable shoes, Federer returned to his favorite stomping grounds at Wimbledon with hopes of turning back the clock one more time.

That opportunity almost never materialized, though, as he needed to rally from two sets down to defeat Julien Benneteau in the third round. It was the eighth time Federer escaped from down two sets to win a match, though he got some help when Benneteau suffered a lower-body injury in the fourth set that robbed him of some mobility (145).

With that crisis averted, Federer finally gained a measure of revenge against Djokovic by defeating him in four sets in the semifinals. It was the first time the two had faced off on grass, and Federer used his wiles to take the starch out of Djokovic's baseline game. It also helped that his service game was on point, and the serve-and-volley Federer of old proved too much for Djokovic to overcome (146).

The reward for Federer's resurgence was a date in the finals opposite Murray, who was carrying the millstone of bidding to become the first Brit to win Wimbledon since Fred Perry in 1936. The pair played two incredibly close opening two sets, splitting them with only one point separating their totals.

A 35-minute rain delay early in the third set proved to be just what Federer needed to create some separation. He took control with a break in the fifth game, finally converting on his sixth such opportunity as he wore down Murray with numerous charges to the net. A break to go up 4-2 in the fourth set was enough space to serve out the match and earn a seventh Wimbledon title.

It moved him into a tie with Sampras and William Renshaw for the most titles won at the all-England club, and he regained the world's number 1 ranking with his 17th Grand Slam. Later that month, he would set the ATP Tour record for most weeks at number 1 with his 286th, bettering Sampras' standard (147).

That title, however, would be Federer's last one until his surprise victory in Melbourne in January. He failed to reach the finals of any Grand Slam in 2013, and his second-round exit at Wimbledon in a loss to Sergiy Stakhovsky was his earliest exit at a major since his first-round loss at the 2003 French Open (148).

Djokovic denied him an eighth Wimbledon title in 2014, winning a five-set thriller in which Federer extended the match by fighting off a championship point in the fourth set as he rallied from 2-5 down to force the decisive fifth. He then missed a chance to go up 4-3 on a break point, and Djokovic took full advantage by closing out the match on Federer's serve for his eighth career Grand Slam title (149).

Djokovic's mastery in the rivalry continued in 2015 when he denied Federer at Wimbledon again, as well as the U.S. Open with four-set victories in both finals. He added a semifinal victory in the 2016 Australian Open semis, and many began to feel the window of opportunity was closing on Federer, who was now 34 years old and battling Father Time as well as opponents (150).

The day after the Australian Open, Federer was running a bath for his twin daughters when he awkwardly shifted weight from his right foot to his left. After a family outing to the zoo in Melbourne, they returned to Switzerland where Federer had an MRI done.

The diagnosis was a torn meniscus in his left knee that would need surgery, and it would knock him out of the French Open. The injury also ended his run of 65 straight Grand Slam appearances dating back to the 2000 Australian Open (151).

He returned in time to compete in Wimbledon, but Milos Raonic ousted him in a five-set battle in the semifinals (152).

By this point, however, the pain in his knee returned because he had come back too soon from his previous knee surgery. Federer consulted with his doctors and opted to shut down completely after Wimbledon to heal properly, which meant no Olympics and no U.S. Open (153).

The decision to rest and recuperate for six months meant that Federer would be 100 percent for the Australian Open. But his absence meant that he dropped event points from the previous year, and as a result, he slid in the ATP Tour rankings to 17th (154).

It was the first time he started the year outside the top 10 since beginning 2002 at number 13. Accordingly, his draw in

Melbourne was a difficult one with four of the top seven players in the world in his half (Murray, Stanislas Wawrinka, Kei Nishikori and Marin Cilic). There was also the unknown that to pertained to Federer himself: how would his surgically repaired knee hold up?

By his usual standards, Federer had lower, yet realistic expectations. He told the local media in Switzerland that reaching the quarterfinals would be a good tournament for him. Oddsmakers had him pegged as a 21-1 shot to win the Australian Open, which was reasonable given that no one could rationally believe Federer would win seven consecutive matches given his layoff and the draw (155).

His opening match against fellow 35-year-old and Austrian Jurgen Melzer was everything one would expect from a player, even a world-class one, after six months away from competitive tennis. Federer mishit balls, played some unsteady and nervous tennis, railed at himself for missed points and shots, and looked inconsistent while trying to find his court legs.

But he also worked his way through those issues to win as he so often has during his career. It was not as much working through the physical issues as it was just allowing himself to ease into mentally focusing on playing again. It all came back so fast for

Federer that he had to pull himself back to relax and start playing tennis (156).

Federer advancing on the first day made for the feel-good moment in Melbourne, but the first shockwave would come shortly after that. Djokovic, the number 2 seed, was stunned in the second round by journeyman and wild-card Denis Istomin. Instantly, one of Federer's primary obstacles was removed, though he would not have seen the Serb until the finals (157).

Federer then recorded a straight-set win over Noah Rubin in the second round, but that would be the last low-profile opponent he would face in Melbourne. Berdych, the 10th seed, awaited in the third round and would likely prove a good measuring stick of just how far along Federer was in his comeback from injury.

Instead, it was Federer who stole the show at Rod Laver Arena with a vintage performance. His serve was tremendous throughout, and the trademark one-handed backhand showed both bite and power. Lastly, Federer showed the needed speed to serve and volley for quick points, and the result was an impressive 6-2, 6-2, 6-4 victory that took just 90 minutes and surprised even Federer himself.

"I didn't expect this as such, to be honest, especially not this kind of scoreline," he said after the match. "I think it was a great mental test for me to see if I could stay in the match point for point. I was able to do that. That's where I'm just really happy that I was able to deliver that," (158).

Federer's portion of his bracket of 16 players held to form, and now number 5 seed Nishikori would be his opponent in the fourth round. Federer held a 4-2 lead in the all-time series between them, but they had not faced each other since the 2015 ATP Tour finals and had never met in a major (159).

Everything that went right for Federer against Berdych turned against him early against Nishikori, who recorded two breaks to race out to a 4-0 lead and eventually won the first set. Federer finally found his stride in the second set thanks to his serve, but it was also his return of serve on Nishikori that proved pivotal.

Federer showed no respect to Nishikori's serve, blasting return winners to flummox the Japanese star. He was charging the net for quick points, and the third set flew by in under a half-hour. Nishikori, though, raised his play in the fourth set and leveled the match by making just three unforced errors.

Nishikori, though, was required to take a medical timeout to treat an ailing hip. While he tried to continue, Federer's arsenal proved too much to overcome as he won the decisive set 6-3 for his 200th victory over a top 10 opponent. Federer nearly doubled the number of winners Nishikori had, racking up an 83-42 advantage (160), but it was the return of his service game that gave him at least a puncher's chance at Grand Slam title number 18.

The draw provided the potential of a Murray-Federer quarterfinal, but Mischa Zverev spoiled those plans by upsetting the number 1 seed in the fourth round. The older brother of teen phenom Alexander Zverev, Mischa was no slouch himself as a top 40 player in the world and proved as such with the biggest win of his career to date (161).

It was the first time Zverev had progressed beyond the third round of a major, while Federer was making his 49th appearance in the final eight of a Grand Slam tournament. The chasm in experience showed itself early as Federer barely broke a sweat in winning the first five games of the match in 13 minutes.

Zverev shook off his disastrous first set to take a 3-1 lead in the second, but Federer refused to let him consolidate the break from the fourth game, breaking back to make it 3-2. The Swiss star poured it on at the end of the second set, winning 11 of the last 13 points to avoid a tiebreak.

In the third set, Federer broke Zverev's will with a pair of well-placed lobs that contributed to a break to go up 3-2 and an eventual straight-set win over the German (162).

In the other half of the bracket, Nadal was also dialing back the years as the ninth seed was making his successful run in Melbourne following some time away due to wrist surgery. He outlasted the younger Zverev in five sets in the third round before beating a pair of top 10 seeds in Monfils (6) and Raonic (3) in the next two rounds to reach the semis (163).

Federer would face compatriot and fourth seed Wawrinka in the semifinals. Wawrinka had finally emerged from out of Federer's long shadow over the first half of the decade. Along with Murray, the two shoehorned their way into discussions over tennis legacies by winning six Grand Slam titles between them.

His first major was the 2014 Australian Open, and Wawrinka was in the semifinals for the third time in four years here. The younger Swiss player was also seeking a second straight Grand Slam title after winning the 2016 U.S. Open.

Federer had won 18 of the previous 21 matches between the two with all three of Wawrinka's victories coming on clay (164). And the first two sets confirmed Federer's supremacy on those faster surfaces as he ran Wawrinka from pillar to post with an array of shots that backed his still dominating serve.

Wawrinka, flustered to the point that he broke his racket against his leg and required a bandage during a medical timeout, suddenly found his groove as Federer lost his serve. Wawrinka won seven straight games, capturing the third set and going up a break in the fourth.

Federer brought the set back on serve with a break of his own at 2-2, but a forehand winner by Wawrinka brought another break at 5-4, and he held serve to force a fifth set.

This time, it was Federer who regrouped by using the medical timeout as he sought treatment for a leg injury that was unrelated to his surgically repaired knee. Those seven minutes calmed Federer down heading into the winner-take-all fifth set.

Federer saved a break point at 1-1 with two great shots after Wawrinka had pinned him to the corner with a punishing backhand, and he gained the all-important break in the sixth game as Wawrinka faltered and double-faulted. Federer was able to serve out the match and advance to his 28th Grand Slam final where he would face either Nadal or 15th-seeded Grigor Dimitrov (165).

But in the end, as it always was for Federer, it would be Nadal in the final. It was the eighth time the two would vie for a Grand Slam title, but it was also the first time that would take place since Nadal won the 2011 French Open in four sets. Nadal had won the previous four Grand Slam finals between the two and entered the match with a 23-11 lead in the all-time rivalry (166).

The first set was a cagey one as both tried to solve the other's game plan. Federer wanted no part of any extended rallies with Nadal given the Spaniard's baseline prowess, and the aggressive net play that had been so successful throughout the tournament was going to continue in the final.

The two stayed on serve until the seventh game when Federer earned two break points as Nadal struggled to find his rhythm. Federer cashed in the first one when Nadal placed a backhand wide and served out the first set with an ace for an early advantage.

Nadal gained an early break in the second set and consolidated it at 3-0 when Federer was unable to put away either of his two opportunities to break back. A second break by Nadal made it 4-0 all but conclusively ended the second set, which the Spaniard won 6-3.

Federer had to dig deep to halt Nadal's momentum and staved off three break points in the first game of the third set with aces on each occasion before Nadal committed two errors to keep the set on serve. Now it was Federer's chance to push ahead with a break point, and he took full advantage to go up 2-0.

Federer's serve continued to amaze as he uncorked his ninth and 10th aces to consolidate the break. At this point, Nadal had no answers for Federer's onslaught, getting broken again to fall behind 1-5 and then wasting two break points as the Swiss star wrapped up the third set with a tidy drop shot while charging the net.

Nadal did not get an opening until the fourth game of the fourth set, converting just his second of 11 break points to take a 3-1 lead. That proved to be too much for Federer to overcome as the two would go to the fifth set of a Grand Slam final for the first time since Nadal's five-set victory at Wimbledon in 2008.

Just like in the semifinals, Federer got medical treatment for his leg before the start of the fifth set. That, however, did not faze Nadal in the slightest as he went up a break in the opening game after Federer pushed an inside-out forehand wide. Nadal consolidated the break in dramatic fashion as he turned away three break points by Federer.

In years past, this would be the point where Federer would seemingly run out of options against Nadal and resign himself to defeat. But this time, Federer stuck with his game plan of attacking the net and using his backhand. There were plenty of occasions where this strategy backfired as Nadal laced sharp-angle passing shots, but he was converting consistently at the net since Nadal's form would occasionally lag.

Federer took a medical timeout before the third game for a quick leg massage and held serve to stay in the match. Nadal saved a break point in the following game with a body blow of a shot, a cross-court two-handed backhand winner that helped him hold serve at 3-1.

Undaunted, Federer continued to charge the net and held serve. He again gained a break point to make it 3-3, only to have Nadal smoke a forehand on Federer's return of service. Nadal had a chance to hold the break, but his backhand clipped the net and fell wide, bringing the game back to deuce.

That reprieve allowed Federer to provide a quality cross-court backhand winner, and after Nadal had tried an inside-out forehand that sailed wide, the final set was back on serve at 3-all. Clearly energized, Federer held serve with a pair of aces in the following game, the second one a bit of a change-up that fooled Nadal to go up 4-3.

Here, Federer sensed blood in the water after Nadal had an unforced error to start the eighth game. He had a forehand winner, and a double fault gave him three break points. Amazingly, though, Nadal regrouped to take them all away, the last coming when Federer mishit Nadal's high-kick second serve.

The match again at deuce, the two engaged in a 26-shot rally, the longest of the game, before Federer fired a forehand winner down the right side for yet another break point. Nadal responded with a service winner down the middle only to have Federer claw out a fifth break point opportunity with a forehand winner.

Finally, Federer converted the break point with one his vintage shots: a majestic one-handed crosscourt backhand from the baseline so perfectly placed that Nadal could not return it. It was now 5-3, and Federer had a chance to serve for the match.

That opportunity, though, started out bleakly as Nadal went up love-30 and had two break points to bring the match back to serve. Federer, though, responded with his 19th ace and then an inside-out forehand winner to push the game to deuce. He got his first championship point when Nadal hit a service return long, but Federer could not put away the match.

A second championship point came after ace number 20. Federer went to his old standby of serve and volley, following it with a forehand smash that looked like it clipped the line at first glance. Nadal challenged the call, and as the crowd anxiously watched the computer's simulated flight of the ball on the screen, they roared when it confirmed the ball was in.

After an initial moment of shock, Federer screamed with delight when it sunk in that he had indeed won his fifth Australian Open title and 18th Grand Slam of his career. Doing so in such unexpected fashion made him savor this one that much more.

"You don't know if they ever come back, these moments," he said. "I told myself to play free. You play the ball. You don't play the opponent. Be free in your head. Be free in your shots. Go for it. The brave will be rewarded here," (167).

Chapter 5: Federer's Rivals

There is not much left to say about Federer's rivalry with Nadal given how much was recounted previously. The statistics of the 35 matches the two have played reveal little about them, save

Federer's early dominance on grass and Nadal's complete mastery on clay.

What the two lack regarding public feuding a la McEnroe and Jimmy Connors they more than compensate for concerning a Borg-McEnroe style elegance and quality to their respective matches against each other. Federer, though, admitted that Nadal's constant pounding of him on clay took a toll psychologically as he pursued the career Grand Slam and chased Sampras' previous high-water mark of 14 major titles.

"The way he played or plays against me has always been extremely difficult for me," he said earlier this year. "I played way too many clay court matches against him. That kind of scarred me. I've really enjoyed watching him, and it's been tough against him, so every match I've won against him I almost count it double for me," (168).

It took Federer six tries on the slower surface to get his first win against Nadal, which came in Hamburg in 2007. All told, Federer is just 2-13 on clay against Nadal with the other victory coming in Madrid in 2009 (169). For all of their matches at Roland Garros and Wimbledon, the two have never played each other at the U.S. Open. This has as much to do with Federer's dominance in New York as much as the rise of first Djokovic and then Murray to land in the opposite half of the bracket as a potential opponent for Nadal.

Still, there is an elegance about the two of them as the pillars of men's tennis that goes back to nearly the start of the 21st century. It was always Roger and Rafa, or Rafa and Roger, depending on the surface. When you combine to win 32 Grand Slam titles as they have, it is hard not to talk about one without quickly adding the other.

While most of Federer's frustrations with Nadal came about because of the Spaniard's on-court brilliance, his rivalry with Djokovic is far more genuine as a clash of two very different personalities. Federer and Djokovic are much like oil and water: they do not mix, and the two are rarely seen in the same circles on the ATP Tour.

Djokovic has always been what could be best labeled as a quirky personality. The casual sports fan knows him for his on-court pranks that include mimicking other players' routines. But there was a point where Djokovic was an immature player during his early days on the circuit, and many thought he quit on matches when things were not going his way.

Federer's history with Djokovic goes back to a 2006 Davis Cup tie between Switzerland and Serbia. Djokovic was facing

Wawrinka, and the two engaged in a five-set match that the Serb won. Federer, though, was incensed over what he felt was Djokovic's constant calling of the trainer during changeovers due to a sinus condition.

It was something that Djokovic eventually required surgery to treat, but at the time, Federer called the constant stalling a "joke" while rallying for his teammate (170). Though both Federer and Djokovic claim they have since moved on from the incident, it has been Djokovic's father who keeps dragging it back to the present.

After criticizing Federer in 2013 to the point where the younger Djokovic apologized publicly, Srdjan Djokovic again went on the offensive in an interview with Newsweek last year. He claimed that Federer, "tried in every possible way to disrespect him because of his breathing problem," and added, "he showed himself to be the best player in the world, but not as a good person at that time," (171).

At the 2009 Australian Open, Federer blistered Djokovic following the Serb's withdrawal of his quarterfinal match against Roddick due to heat illness while trailing two sets to one and 2-1 in the fourth set. For the low-key Federer, going public with such pointed words raised a lot of eyebrows on the tour.

"I'm almost in favor of saying, you know what, if you're not fit enough, just get out of here," he said at the time. "If Novak were up two sets to love, I don't think he would have retired 4-0 down in the fourth. Thanks to Andy that he retired in the end. Andy pushed him to the limits. Hats off to Andy," (172).

On the court, though, Federer and Djokovic have played some stirring tennis at times. Federer won the first four matches between the two before Djokovic broke through at the final of the 2007 Toronto Masters final. They have met in four Grand Slam finals, with Djokovic winning the last three after Federer bested him at the 2007 U.S. Open.

But the 2011 U.S. Open semifinal in which Djokovic won following his "Forehand Heard 'Round the World" was a turning point of sorts. Including that match, the Serb has emerged victorious in 15 of the 23 games between the two. Federer has lost five of six Grand Slam matches to Djokovic in that span, all either semifinals or finals (173).

Despite their contrasting personalities, three things bond Federer and Djokovic: Tennis, a career Grand Slam, and more recently for Djokovic, trying to raise a family. Djokovic's upset at the Australian Open and subsequent revelation that he was struggling to balance work and family came across as surprising, but not surprising when you read into Federer's thoughts on the subject since he spoke from personal experience.

"Novak is going through a crisis, and it surprised me," he said. "But once you realize career Grand Slam, a new career begins. You have to ask yourself, why do I keep playing? You have to change your mentality, what are your goals? Sometimes it requires a week, sometimes a month, a year, or you do not find the right feeling anymore," (174).

Playing Djokovic and Nadal over the years has been akin to trench warfare: attack and counter and attack and counter until one side gives up due to physical and mental exhaustion. For Federer, facing Murray provides a respite from those grim baseline slugfests since the Scot shares many of the same diverse on-court qualities as the Swiss.

Murray also does not have the polarizing personality of Djokovic or the "wow" factor of Nadal. He is, for lack of a better term, quintessentially British in persona and demeanor. Of the five current players to win multiple Grand Slam titles, none of the other four have had any personal clashes with Murray.

There is an understood respect, both publicly and privately, that Federer and other players have for Murray. That is because his burden of carrying the hopes and dreams of British tennis, like Henman before him, is unique to any player on the ATP Tour. And it can be argued that it is an unfair one.

Murray entered the ATP Tour full-time right around Federer's peak in the middle of the 2000s. While Nalbandian was a peer who came up with Federer in juniors, Murray was in the same circles as Djokovic, but unlike the Serb, Murray quickly figured out Federer's game.

Murray won six of the first eight matches between the two, though Federer won the most important one with a straight-set triumph at the 2008 U.S. Open finals. It was Murray's first Grand Slam final, and he continued to charge at the door repeatedly in a bid to turn the "Big Three" of Federer, Nadal, and Djokovic into the "Big Four" (175).

Federer turned him away at both the 2010 Australian Open and the 2012 Wimbledon finals, leaving Murray winless in four tries to win a Grand Slam title (176). Losing Wimbledon was a particularly cruel blow for Murray, whose levels of acceptance in England often hinge on his levels of success. When he wins, he is British. When he loses, he is Scottish.

The two had split 16 lifetime matches before Murray had his most significant breakthrough by defeating Federer in the gold medal match of the 2012 Olympics in London. If the venue had been anywhere but the all-England club, it may have lacked some of the psychological heft it had been assigned for Murray's hopes beyond the gold medal, but during a summer where team Great Britain had wildly overachieved during the games, Murray did his part to keep the party going.

Only a month prior, Murray was reduced to tears by Federer as the burden of being Britain's savior started noticeably wearing on him. But he made the gold a priority, and it was also something Federer had never claimed in singles. Federer also had to deal with a nation in Murray's corner.

This was not unfamiliar to Federer after all his previous trips to Wimbledon, but the ferocity and intensity in which the partisan and patriotic crowd backed the Scot was.

Murray won the first set and was up 2-0 in the second before the two engaged in a 15-minute struggle the next game. Federer had six break points, and Murray beat back every one of them to the delight of the crowd.

He won the second set, and after Murray broke Federer midway through the third for a 4-1 lead, the moment a nation had desperately longed for finally had arrived, because Murray had finally arrived as well.

"Andy had a clear plan," Federer said afterward, "and never looked like he was doubting himself" (177).

Federer, though, has won six of the eight matches since the Olympic defeat to gain a 14-11 lead in the all-time series. But Murray did knock him out of the 2014 Australian Open in the quarterfinals, and with three majors under his belt, they are on equal footing for the rest of Federer's career (178).

It is hard to call Federer and Wawrinka a rivalry when the record is so lopsided in Federer's favor. Two of the three clay-court wins for Wawrinka have come at the Monte Carlo Masters, and the other the 2015 French Open semifinals (179). And while the two have been Davis Cup teammates for Switzerland for over a decade, they have also been at odds with each other.

The most public row between Federer and Wawrinka came at the 2014 ATP World Tour finals, which is the year-ending tournament on the tour for the eight highest-ranked players. It was a big year for Wawrinka, who had won the Australian Open for his first Grand Slam title and had moved ahead of Federer in the player rankings for the first time in his career.

Federer and Wawrinka were placed in opposite groups for the round-robin and met in the semifinals. The two waged a tense contest with Federer rallying from a set down and holding off four match points to defeat Wawrinka in a third-set tiebreak. But any ideas of this being a friendly match between the two Swiss was turned on its head during a changeover in which Wawrinka argued with members of Federer's entourage in the crowd at deuce while Federer was serving at 5-5.

Federer had denied Wawrinka three times at match point at 4-5 and again at 5-6 in the tiebreak before winning the final three points, closing out the match with a drop shot that Wawrinka could only helplessly watch from the baseline (180).

Federer withdrew from the final against Djokovic, citing a bad back, but shortly after that was announced, the British media came forth with claims that Wawrinka was arguing with Federer's wife during that deuce at 5-5 after Mirka had accused Wawrinka of "whingeing" while trying to serve for the match (181).

That reportedly prompted Federer and Wawrinka to have a 10-minute argument after the match at the O2 Arena, though neither of them commented directly on the incident with the media post-match (182).

But both were forced to address the issue, at least indirectly, the following day when an Irish newspaper provided confirmation from the match judge that Mirka did indeed tweak Wawrinka at that pivotal point in the match, and video footage backed the umpire's assertions.

The two downplayed the tete-a-tete at a Davis Cup press conference, with Federer admitting there was a conversation after the match and adding, "We are having a good time here – we are friends, not enemies. He had a big a moment, a situation, but everyone has done a nice job of making it really big," (183).

With Wawrinka in his early 30s, there is little chance that he will put a sizable dent in his deficit of head-to-head meetings with Federer. But Wawrinka has a chance to complete a career Grand Slam if he can win Wimbledon. The grass has never been overly kind to Wawrinka, whose quarterfinal appearances in 2014 and 2015 represented his high-water marks at the all-England club.

Wawrinka, though, has beaten the best to win his three majors. He topped Nadal in Melbourne and Djokovic in both Paris and New York, making him someone whom Federer will not take lightly (184).

Chapter 6: Personal Life

One of the things that has always stood out about Roger Federer on the court is his emotional nature. In his youth, it was his anger at his failures, but for the better part of 15 years now, when Federer is emotional after a match, it is usually crying tears of joy after a hard-earned victory and lifting yet another Grand Slam trophy.

The adage of "behind every good man there is a woman," certainly holds true in the case of Federer and his wife, Mirka. Like her husband and Federer's parents before her, Mirka Federer was a pretty good tennis player. She climbed as high as number 76 in the WTA Tour rankings and won three ITF titles in singles and one in doubles (185).

Originally a native of Czechoslovakia, the Vavrinec family moved to Switzerland when Mirka was two. Her love of tennis was instilled at an early age following a meeting with all-time women's great Martina Navratilova at the age of nine while in Germany.

Like her husband, Mirka won a Swiss title as a junior during her teenage years, and she first met Federer in 1997. Her playing career, though, was cut short by a foot injury, and her best showing at a Grand Slam event was reaching the third round of the U.S. Open in 2001.

The two had started dating the previous year at the Olympics when they both represented Switzerland at the Sydney Games.

Mirka lost in the first round in both singles and doubles for the Swiss while Federer lost the bronze-medal match to France's Arnaud Di Pasquale in singles as their careers began diverging in different directions.

"We spent two weeks together, that's how we got to know each other, and on the last day before we left, we kissed for the first time in Sydney," Roger recounted (186).

Their relationship grew both personally and professionally. Mirka became part of Roger's business team and was in charge of his schedule and dealings with the media while his parents dealt with the finances.

Her familiarity with the tennis lifestyle provided Roger one less distraction in chasing his on-court dreams. The two shared a flat in Wimbledon in 2003 when Federer won his first Grand Slam title, and later that year they moved in together in a suburb near Basel (187).

But being Federer's business manager and girlfriend did cause speculation at times. She hit back at former Wimbledon champion Pat Cash in 2004 after the Australian accused Mirka of having a "Svengali-like grip" on Federer in a column following the decision to part ways with Lundgren (188).

It was classic he said, she said fodder for the Australian tabloids and Mirka provided plenty of fodder going up against one of the country's beloved tennis icons.

"I think that Cash should just shut up," she said in responding to his comments. "It hurts when someone says things like this, and I don't know where he got these ideas because I don't know him and I haven't met him.

"Maybe if I was a crazy, disco-dancing girl who dragged him away to go shopping all the time after having known him for just a year, then Cash's comments may have been understood. But I am the complete opposite of that," (189).

Federer also backed his wife in that interview, stating that everything Cash had written was untrue and that "as long as that's the case, I cannot take it seriously," (190).

While the two were rarely seen together in public in the early part of their relationship, a decision by mutual choice, Mirka became a fixture in Federer's box cheering for her boyfriend, and eventually, her husband. Now and then she would be his hitting partner as the two traveled together, but she was always his best friend in addition to his girlfriend.

The two were married in April 2009, and Mirka gave birth to twin girls Myla and Charlene three months later. They were recently joined by another set of twins, this time boys Leo and Lenny in 2014.

It's easy to view Mirka as the woman who is often seen, but never heard. She has shared those court boxes with plenty of celebrities, from Vogue magazine editor Anna Wintour to pop stars Gwen Stefani and Gavin Rossdale. But to overlook her is to ignore the character she has helped instill within Roger Federer that has propelled him to those 18 Grand Slam titles.

"She loves this life," Wintour said in one of her few statements on subjects outside of the fashion world. "She is happy to set up the houses, look after the twins, and maybe have more children. And she also knows she makes this career possible," (191).

The 2014 incident with Wawrinka, though, cast her in a different light. While both Roger and Wawrinka tried to diffuse the situation with a united front at their Davis Cup news conference, it was highly out of character for Mirka to cheer against one of Roger's opponents as opposed to cheering for her husband.

But as Federer's career fully enters its final act, it is the actual adventure that appeals to him most in addition to winning. It is now traveling as a family of six, though it can be argued it is more like a village when you include nannies for all four children and tutors for his eldest daughters.

It is about visiting the ATP Tour events off the beaten path, such as Turkey and India. Yes, they provide exorbitant appearance fees for Federer on top of the prize money he could win, but it is the chance to find new life experiences as the number of tournaments slowly count down to his eventual retirement that holds an allure.

"The girls enjoy it, and I love being with my family, and so does Mirka," he said. "She loves being with me, so we get to see each other every single day, basically, and I think that's more important than being apart from each other and them going to normal school at the moment," (192).

It also seems that the time off in 2016 following his knee surgery did both of them some good. They appear liberated of being self-conscious of their surroundings. Mirka caused a comical stir in Melbourne with what could best be described as a garish pink Gucci sweater with green trim for Federer's semifinal match against Wawrinka.

Given how sartorially splendid Roger is on and off the court, the brash colors of Mirka's sweater caused Twitter to publicly weigh in on if the $2,000 top was a fashion do or do not (193).

Federer's success has also put him in high demand for commercial endorsements. He has been the pitchman for everything from Rolex watches to Moet champagne and a few things in between, most notably Nike, Mercedes-Benz, and Gillette. His friendship with Wintour started in 2010 since she was not a stranger to the U.S. Open scene (194).

The two managed to make tennis a trendy place to experiment with fashion on the men's side, something Serena and Venus Williams and Maria Sharapova were doing for women's outfits. Federer accompanied Wintour to Milan for Fashion Week, something he said "was the most incredible few days of my life" (195).

The headstrong Federer from his teenage years is still that demanding perfectionist on the court, but his family life has mellowed him off it outside those rectangular lines. It is hard to find anyone in the sport who has a bad word to say about Federer or even having a bad interaction with him.

His grounded persona makes him accessible to the everyday tennis fan. Federer has never been afraid to recount his self-doubts publicly, and his ability to hold court on subjects beyond tennis makes him a media darling.

With that public persona comes the opportunity for philanthropy, and Federer has made an impact in this area as well. He helped found the Roger Federer Foundation, with its primary stated goal of helping African children in poverty gain access to high-quality early learning and education.

The foundation claims to have impacted more than 600,000 children and hopes to reach one million by 2018. What makes his organization distinctive is that it seeks to motivate people to organize and develop skills to find the needed resources as opposed to just delivering a product to people (196).

In 2015, the foundation raised more than 5.6 million Swiss francs in donations while spending nearly 5 million to its causes. The figure is impressive considering there were no high-profile fundraisers attached to the charity for the year. It also had approximately 15 million Swiss francs in assets according to its 2015 report (197).

Chapter 7: Roger Federer's Impact

When Roger Federer finally decides to hang up his tennis sneakers and racket, there will be a hole in men's tennis that will be next to impossible to fill. His lengthy track record of success at the highest levels to secure his status as an all-time great, or more likely, the greatest of all-time, has already been cemented.

But what comes next for tennis? His contrasting styles with Nadal and Djokovic and his similarities with Murray make plenty of fodder for debate over which style will win out in the future and what form the next superstar player who can make a run at Federer's total of 18 major titles will utilize.

Kids who pull up old Federer matches on YouTube will see a player who had no glaring weaknesses. He had a full toolbox of options at his disposal to beat an opponent. Let us go through the checklist:

Big serve? Absolutely. Federer could line up his first serve with anyone when it came to speed and power, but also placement in the box. And much the way a quality baseball pitcher can throw all his pitches with the same arm motion and slot angle, Federer can disguise the various types of serve in the form of one smooth movement that pushed a ball wide or handcuffed a player's wrists to his body in an attempt to return that serve.

Powerful forehand? Yes. While it lacked the brute force and cumulative punishment of Nadal's groundstrokes, Federer's forehand was still a force. Any lack of power was well-hidden by his exceptionally quick wrists that helped him drive through shots in a fundamentally sound way. Federer could place his forehand anywhere he wanted to, whether to pull it down either line or slap it inside-out crosscourt.

Backhand? Much the way Steffi Graf drove opponents on crazy on the women's side with a slice backhand, Federer did likewise as part of his peerless game on grass and high-quality play on clay. It was a stroke that required nearly a decade to hone. But what separated Federer was the power he generated with his one-handed backhand, hitting the ball earlier in its trajectory with a flatter stroke (198).

His confidence in sticking with this shot was a key reason he defeated Nadal in Melbourne in January, and it could prove useful again at the remaining three majors of 2017.

Speed and footwork? Here is an underrated feature of Federer's game. When one watches his 2003 Wimbledon rout of Philippoussis, two things stand out. The first is his ability to hit through the ball on either side with tremendous power. The second is his ability to cover side to side on the baseline to be in a position to hit through the ball to set up those winners.

Federer rarely looks fast on the court since he utilizes an entire economy of motion that gets him into position. If he has to turn on the afterburners to track down a shot, he can. But seldom was there a time, especially in the prime of his career, that he was unable to return a shot because he was too slow.

Tactics? It is one thing to have the physical tools to be an elite tennis player, but it is nearly impossible to win unless the mental ones are there as well. Federer's drive is not unique to tennis. Every player who reaches the ATP Tour has the drive that propels them to be a professional, but the intensity of Federer's drive is distinctive.

There were various points throughout this decade where the media have written off Federer as first Nadal, then Djokovic, and later Murray had overtaken the Swiss maestro and added Grand Slam titles to their trophy cases while Federer remained stuck on 17. His hiring of boyhood idol Edberg in 2014 was a concession to their improved play but also a note of defiance that he could rediscover that lost form.

The two worked on the philosophy of quick points and more net play to blunt the power of Nadal and Djokovic. It met with mixed results and no Grand Slam titles, though 2016 could be chalked up as a lost year given Federer's two knee surgeries.

The reality was that he probably came back too soon at Wimbledon, semifinal appearance notwithstanding.

To have the bravery to take an extended period off at 35 was a risk few would consider, let alone embrace. But it allowed Federer to reset physically and mentally, with the latter at his age being more important since the mind makes the body willing to survive a fortnight of grueling tennis.

Federer made his observations through playing the Australian Open, how he had to ramp up his mental focus as opposed to just throwing himself into every point as a life-and-death struggle (199).

He also had to have confidence in his approach, which is a difficult thing when staring across the court at a player who has not only seen your best but repeatedly dismantled it in soul-crushing methods.

Federer will savor every title a little more going forward because he was rewarded for staying on the path in Melbourne. It would have been easy to throw in the towel at 1-2 after squandering a break point and again at 2-3, and it would have been easier to say the hell with tactics and just go for broke.

His drive reunited with patience and persistence against Nadal. And if any player from the next generation can discover that at a young age, that is the player most likely to make a run to be the next great player of men's tennis.

Federer's impact, however, goes just beyond the mere game of tennis. He served as president of the ATP Tour Player Council from 2008-14, providing a voice for not only the elite players but those further down in the rankings in a bid to grow the sport in the always-competitive world of the sports entertainment dollar.

He pushed for the majors to have a larger share of revenue be prize money for the players and addressed a distribution gap in that prize money by trying to get tournaments to make a greater percentage available in earlier rounds (200). Federer also laid the groundwork for succeeding president Eric Butorac to renegotiate the prize money allotment for the Masters Series tournaments, which are high-caliber tournaments a step below the Grand Slams (201).

There was also progress on some lesser-publicized areas, such as the more extensive use of bio-passports to help guard against blood doping and more frequent in-season drug tests (202).

Federer was clearly a good player who was good for the game, but his lasting impact may also provide the biggest challenge to the sport: who will pick up the mantle to be the next Roger Federer?

If Federer and his merry band of 30-somethings on the ATP Tour are still going to not only be competitive but keep winning Grand Slam titles, where does that leave the generation behind them? Advances in racket technology have not only lengthened careers, they have assimilated the surfaces to the point where the talent gap has been compressed at varying levels (203).

Surfaces are also slower regardless of type, even the hard court. The advantage seems to have swung favor to a defensive brand of tennis. Djokovic is probably the best player currently at this tactic, and it will be interesting to see if that theory holds true if the "Big Four" of Federer, Nadal, Djokovic and Murray all end up together in the semifinals of any tournament.

Chapter 8: Roger Federer's Legacy

When Nadal's video challenge on match point failed to overturn Federer's winner on match point in Melbourne in January 2017, Federer's legacy changed profoundly. The resulting swing of this Australian Open title in which Federer extended his lead in majors over Nadal to four instead of the Spaniard reducing the deficit to two made it that much harder to deny Federer's place as the best player of at least his generation.

And there is plenty of room to add all-time to the argument. Federer is one of only eight players to complete the career Grand Slam, and he played against three of them in Nadal, Djokovic, and Agassi. Though Federer had limited exposure to Sampras and Agassi given the timelines of their respective career, Nadal and Djokovic have been his peers his entire career and combined with him to put a stranglehold on men's singles.

The consistency and longevity of Federer's success in Grand Slam events are unequaled and another feather in his cap for the argument of being the greatest all-time. He reached the semifinals or finals of 23 consecutive Grand Slam events from 2004-10 and at least the quarterfinals of 36 straight Grand Slam tournaments until his shocking second-round exit at Wimbledon in 2013.

By comparison, Nadal's longest run of Slam semifinals or finals appearances is five. His longest run of reaching the final eight in such events is 11. Additionally, injuries resulted in his absence from five Grand Slam tournaments from 2009 through last year. It was only last year that Federer succumbed to a knee injury that marked his first absence from a Grand Slam since failing to get out of the qualifying draw for the 1999 U.S. Open.

Djokovic has shown the ability to match Federer's consistency in success and longevity at points in his career, reaching the semifinals or finals of 14 successive Grand Slam events from 2010-13. Including quarterfinals, that number becomes 28 spanning the 2009 Wimbledon tournament until his 3rd-round exit from last year's event at the all-England club.

Federer's hold on the number 1 ranking on the ATP Tour for 237 consecutive weeks from 2004-08 is another record that could stand the test of time similar to Joe DiMaggio's 56-game hitting streak in Major League Baseball in 1941. The next closest player is Jimmy Connors at 160, and Sampras' longest run atop the rankings was 102.

Federer's overall mark of 302 weeks at number 1 could be challenged by Djokovic, who is currently at 223. The Serbian also had a run of 122 weeks at number 1, which ended last November when he was overtaken by Andy Murray.

While Nadal and Djokovic are the closest pursuers to Federer's 18 titles, there is no guarantee either will pass the Swiss star. Given Nadal's form in Melbourne, he will be considered one of the favorites at Roland Garros in chasing his record ninth French Open title. Moving ahead of Sampras with his 15th Grand Slam title, though, would indirectly add heft to the argument of Federer's greatness.

Djokovic, though, is more of a wild card when it comes to Federer's legacy. The Serb's star was clearly in the ascendancy over the past four years, highlighted by his "Djokovic slam" from 2015-16 in which he held all four Grand Slam titles simultaneously and moved into fourth place with 12 for his career. Being one of only three players to win four consecutive Grand Slam tournaments, calendar year or otherwise is an accomplishment Federer is unlikely to equal.

But since completing his own career Grand Slam with the 2016 French Open title, Djokovic has struggled to recapture that form. He made a third-round exit at Wimbledon trying to win that event for a third straight year and lost in the U.S. Open final to

Wawrinka. But it was his second-round loss to Istomin in Melbourne this year that caught everyone's attention.

The rumblings and rumors that family, and not tennis, is Djokovic's top priority after his quick Melbourne walkabout raised eyebrows. The narrative runs directly contrary to the single-minded focus and drive that has defined Djokovic in recent years as he turned the era of the "Big Two" of Federer and Nadal into the "Big Three" with his success.

Now that success, at least on an elite level, may come with an expiration date for the Serb. His play in both Masters Series events, as well as this year's Grand Slams, may provide tell-tale clues regarding his desire to try and make up the distance between himself and both Nadal and Federer.

Federer had his chances on two occasions to hold all four titles simultaneously, but Nadal snuffed out both of them at Roland Garros in 2006 and 2007. These are just two of his ten losses in Grand Slam finals; a statistic that further bolsters those backing Federer as the greatest of all-time. He has made 28 Grand Slam finals, with Djokovic and Nadal tied for a distant second with 21.

It is an argument similar to Jack Nicklaus' label as the greatest golfer of all time: In addition to his 18 majors, Nicklaus finished in sole possession of second place on 11 other occasions (204).

Federer's ten finals losses trail only Ivan Lendl's 11, and nine of them came to either Nadal (6) or Djokovic (3). There is strength in the argument over the lack of depth on the ATP Tour until the rise of Murray and more recently, Wawrinka, since 2012, but there is also no denying the tour had never seen three players operate at such an elite level for such a prolonged period.

And the trio's dominance ensured Murray and Wawrinka, currently the only other players with multiple Grand Slam titles to their names, will never catch Federer, Nadal, or Djokovic. As the next generation of stars tries to make headway against this old guard, no one player stands out as so dominant as to pose a threat to Federer's mark.

The leading candidate may be 19-year-old Alexander Zverev of Germany. Currently the youngest player ranked in the Top 50 of the ATP Tour and on the cusp of the top 20, Zverev took Nadal to five sets in the third round of the Australian Open and defeated Federer in the semifinals in Halle, Germany, last summer.

Zverev broke through for his first ATP Tour win last fall in St. Petersburg, Russia, defeating Tomas Berdych and Wawrinka in the final two rounds. In his first full circuit of Grand Slam events in 2016, Zverev reached the third round at both the French Open and Wimbledon and the second round of the U.S. Open. He lost to Murray in straight sets in the opening round of the 2016 Australian Open (205).

Still, Zverev's time is not likely to come for a few years. But it will have to come soon to have any chance of potentially catching Federer, whose 2003 Wimbledon title came at the age of 21. The ATP Tour has labeled Zverev as one of its "Next Generation" stars (206), so it will be curious to see if he can live up to the hype.

It is difficult to conjure up an argument against Federer's status as the greatest of all-time. Nadal and Djokovic both deserve immense credit for evolving both their style of play and their level of play to match, and at times exceed Federer. To that regard, Nadal may be the more impressive of the two given his early stature of being solely a baseline basher who has dominated the red clay of Roland Garros like no other.

The Spaniard willed himself into being a better player to challenge and defeat Federer on his best surface at Wimbledon while staying true to his fundamental strengths. And given his strong winning percentage head-to-head against Federer, it's hard to deny Nadal his due.

Djokovic possesses an all-around game that is comparable to Federer, and he has been the top player of this current decade with 10 Grand Slam titles and six runner-up finishes. The Serb and Swiss have styles that mirror each other, and at times have had the same prickly demeanor that gives their rivalry some off-court gristle as well as on-court fireworks.

But when one looks at the overall picture of men's tennis, the title of best rightfully belongs to Federer. Eighteen Grand Slam titles, 28 Grand Slam finals appearances, a career Grand Slam and the length of his elite consistency at those tournaments have created a standard all others have yet to match.

The 35-year-old still has room in the trophy case for one or maybe even two more Grand Slam titles if his body can hold up over the next two years. Like his victory in Melbourne, it may take a little bit of luck on his part as well as a little bit of luck in the draw with any one of the remaining "Big Five" making an early exit over the course of a fortnight. But make no mistake, Federer is most certainly a threat to add to his already record haul.

And any such victories would just add to the legacy that is Roger Federer.

Final Word/About the Author

I was born and raised in Norwalk, Connecticut. Growing up, I could often be found spending many nights watching basketball, soccer, and football matches with my father in the family living room. I love sports and everything that sports can embody. I believe that sports are one of most genuine forms of competition, heart, and determination. I write my works to learn more about influential athletes in the hopes that from my writing, you the reader can walk away inspired to put in an equal if not greater amount of hard work and perseverance to pursue your goals. If you enjoyed *Roger Federer: The Inspiring Story of One of Tennis' Greatest Legends,* please leave a review! Also, you can read more of my works on *Novak Djokovic, Andrew Luck, Rob Gronkowski, Brett Favre, Calvin Johnson, Drew Brees, J.J. Watt, Colin Kaepernick, Aaron Rodgers, Peyton Manning, Tom Brady, Russell Wilson, Michael Jordan, LeBron James, Kyrie Irving, Klay Thompson, Stephen Curry, Kevin Durant, Russell Westbrook, Anthony Davis, Chris Paul, Blake Griffin, Kobe Bryant, Joakim Noah, Scottie Pippen, Carmelo Anthony, Kevin Love, Grant Hill, Tracy McGrady, Vince Carter, Patrick Ewing, Karl Malone, Tony Parker, Allen Iverson, Hakeem Olajuwon, Reggie Miller, Michael Carter-Williams, John Wall, James Harden, Tim Duncan, Steve Nash, Draymond Green, Kawhi*

Leonard, Dwyane Wade, Ray Allen, Pau Gasol, Dirk Nowitzki, Jimmy Butler, Paul Pierce, Manu Ginobili, Pete Maravich, Larry Bird, Kyle Lowry, Jason Kidd, David Robinson, LaMarcus Aldridge, Derrick Rose, Paul George, Kevin Garnett, Chris Paul, Marc Gasol, Yao Ming, Al Horford and Amar'e Stoudemire in the Kindle Store. If you love basketball, check out my website at claytongeoffreys.com to join my exclusive list where I let you know about my latest books and give you lots of goodies.

Like what you read? Please leave a review!

I write because I love sharing the stories of influential people like Roger Federer with fantastic readers like you. My readers inspire me to write more so please do not hesitate to let me know what you thought by leaving a review! If you love books on life, basketball, or productivity, check out my website at claytongeoffreys.com to join my exclusive list where I let you know about my latest books. Aside from being the first to hear about my latest releases, you can also download a free copy of *33 Life Lessons: Success Principles, Career Advice & Habits of Successful People*. See you there!

Clayton

References

I.   Stauffer, Rene. "The Roger Federer Story: Quest for Perfection." 2006. E-book. 3.

II.   Stauffer 3.

III.   Stauffer 4.

IV.   Stauffer 5.

V.   Stauffer 6.

VI.   Stauffer 6.

VII.   Stauffer 6.

VIII.   Stauffer 8.

IX.   Stuaffer 8.

X.   Stauffer 9.

XI.   Stauffer 9.

XII.   Stauffer 10.

XIII.   Stauffer 10.

XIV.   Stauffer 11.

XV.   Stauffer 11-12.

XVI.   Stauffer 13.

XVII.   Stauffer 14.

XVIII. Stauffer 14-15.

XIX. Stauffer 17.

XX. Stauffer 17.

XXI. Stauffer 18.

XXII. Stauffer 18.

XXIII. Stauffer 21.

XXIV. Stauffer 21.

XXV. Stauffer 22.

XXVI. Stauffer 22.

XXVII. Stauffer 23.

XXVIII. Stauffer 23.

XXIX. Stauffer 24.

XXX. Stauffer 25.

XXXI. "Like Nick Kyrgios, Roger Federer Also Tanked During A Pro Tennis Match." 7 July 2015. World Tennis Magazine. Web.

XXXII. Stauffer 25.

XXXIII. Stauffer 33.

XXXIV. Stauffer 33.

XXXV. Stauffer 33.

XXXVI. Stauffer 35.

XXXVII.   Stauffer 35.

XXXVIII.   "Marcelo Rios Bio." ATP Tour. Web.

XXXIX.   "Roger Federer's Rankings History." ATP Tour. Web.

XL.   "Roger Federer Player Activity." ATP Tour. Web.

XLI.   "Roger Federer Player Activity." ATP Tour. Web.

XLII.   "Roger Federer Player Activity." ATP Tour. Web.

XLIII.   Stauffer 42.

XLIV.   "Roger Federer Player Activity." ATP Tour. Web.

XLV.   "Roger Federer Player Activity." ATP Tour. Web.

XLVI.   "Roger Federer Player Activity." ATP Tour. Web.

XLVII. "Federer Ends Sampras Reign." 2 July 2001. BBC Sport. Web.

XLVIII.   Allen, J.A. "Roger Federer vs. Pete Sampras 2001: Remaking the Wimbledon Classic in 2010." 1 July 2010. Bleacher Report. Web.

XLIX.   "Roger Federer Player Activity." ATP Tour. Web.

L.   "Roger Federer Player Activity." ATP Tour. Web.

LI.   Swanton, Will. "Peter Carter: The coach who molded Roger Federer." 1 September 2012. The Australian. Web.

LII.   Swanton.

LIII.   Swanton.

LIV.   "Roger Federer Player Activity." ATP Tour. Web.

LV.   "Roger Federer Player Activity." ATP Tour. Web.

LVI.   "Roger Federer Player Activity." ATP Tour. Web.

LVII.   "Lleyton Hewitt Player Activity." ATP Tour. Web.

LVIII.   "Roger Federer Player Activity." ATP Tour. Web.

LIX.   "Roger Federer Player Activity." ATP Tour. Web.

LX.   "Roger Federer Player Activity." ATP Tour. Web.

LXI.   "Feliciano Lopez Player Activity." ATP Tour. Web.

LXII.   "Roger Federer Player Activity." ATP Tour. Web.

LXIII.   "Roger Federer Player Activity." ATP Tour. Web.

LXIV.   "Roger Federer vs. Andy Roddick Head 2 Head." ATP Tour. Web.

LXV.   "Federer destroys Roddick." 4 July 2003. BBC Sport. Web.

LXVI.   "Overview of Match Stats between Roger Federer and Andy Roddick." 4 July 2003. ATP Tour. Web.

LXVII. Clarey, Christopher. "Australian Beats Agassi at Wimbledon with 46 Aces." 30 June 2003. The New York Times. Web.

LXVIII.   "Head 2 Head Mark Philippoussis vs. Roger Federer." 6 July 2003. ATP Tour. Web.

LXIX.   "Wimbledon Final 2003 – Federer vs. Philippoussis – FULL MATCH." 19 January 2017. YouTube via TENNIS TROPHY. Web.

LXX. "Roger Federer Rankings History." ATP Tour. Web.

LXXI. "Roger Federer Player Activity." ATP Tour. Web.

LXXII. Bierley, Stephen. "Federer leads revolution from the front." 1 February 2004. The Guardian. Web.

LXXIII. Henderson, Jon. "Kuerten magic floors Federer." 29 May 2004. The Guardian. Web.

LXXIV. "Andy Roddick Player Activity." ATP Tour. Web.

LXXV. Newbery, Piers. "Federer fights back to retain title." 4 July 2004. BBC Sport. Web.

LXXVI. "Roger Federer Player Activity." ATP Tour Web.

LXXVII. Robbins, Liz. "Federer is Too Much for Hewitt in U.S. Open Final." 13 September 2004. The New York Times. Web.

LXXVIII. "Federer survives Agassi fightback." 9 Setpember 2004. CNN International. Web.

LXXIX. Robbins.

LXXX. "Roger Federer Player Activity." ATP Tour. Web.

LXXXI. "Roger Federer Player Activity." ATP Tour. Web.

LXXXII. "Nadal Shocks Federer at French Open." 4 June 2005. China Daily. Web.

LXXXIII. China Daily.
LXXXIV. Clarey, Christopher. "Federer (Yawn) Wins at Wimbledon Again." 4 July 2005. The New York Times. Web.

LXXXV.   Clarke, Liz. "Federer is 'Just Too Good' For Agassi in Open Final." 12 September 2005. Washington Post. Web.

LXXXVI.   "Roger Federer Player Activity." ATP Tour. Web.

LXXXVII.   Bierley, Steve. "Tears for fabulous Federer and fears for every rival." 30 January 2006. The Guardian. Web.

LXXXVIII.   Bierley.

LXXXIX.   Buddell, James. "Rafa vs. Roger, The Match That Cemented Their Rivalry." 15 May 2016. ATP Tour. Web.

XC.   "Nadal ends Federer dream in Paris." 11 June 2006. BBC Sport. Web.

XCI.   Bierley, Steve. "Federer takes crown for a fourth year but Nadal leaves his nerves in shreds." 10 July 2006. The Guardian. Web.

XCII.   Newbery, Piers. "Federer battles to fourth crown." 9 July 2006. BBC Sport. Web.

XCIII.   Clarey, Christopher. "Federer in a Class by Himself." 11 September 2006. The New York Times. Web.

XCIV.   "Roger Federer Player Activity." ATP Tour. Web.

XCV.   "Roger Federer Player Activity." ATP Tour. Web.

XCVI.   "Federer perfect in winning Australian Open." 28 January 2007. ESPN.com. Web.

XCVII. ESPN.com.

XCVIII.   "Roger Federer Player Activity." ATP Tour. Web.

XCIX.   Federer ends Nadal's clay streak." 20 May 2007. BBC Sport. Web.

C.   Macur, Juliet. "Nadal Defeats Federer for French Open Title." 11 June 2007. The New York Times. Web.

CI.   "Roger Federer Player Activity." ATP Tour. Web.

CII.   Branch, John. "Federer Wins His Fifth Wimbledon Title in a Row." 9 July 2007. The New York Times. Web.

CIII.   "Federer matches Borg record." 9 July 2007. The Guardian. Web.

CIV.   "Roger Federer Player Activity." ATP Tour. Web.

CV.   Newbery, Piers. "World number one Roger Federer won a fourth consecutive U.S. Open title with a hard-fought victory over Novak Djokovic." 9 September 2007. BBC Sport. Web.

CVI.   "Roger Federer Player Activity." ATP Tour. Web.

CVII.   "Roger Federer Player Activity." ATP Tour. Web.

CVIII. Ford, Bonnie D. "Nadal's fire and emotion propel him to fourth French Open title." 9 June 2008. ESPN.com. Web.

CIX.   "Roger Federer Player Activity." ATP Tour. Web.

CX.   "Rafael Nadal Player Activity." ATP Tour. Web.

CXI.   "Federer vs Nadal Wimbledon 2008 Final: The greatest Tie Break of all time." 26 May 2014. BestofTennis via YouTube. Web.

CXII.   Martin, Dave. "Reliving 2008 Wimbledon Final: The Greatest Match Ever." 1 September 2015. The Epoch Times. Web.

CXIII. "Rafael Nadal Rankings History." ATP Tour. Web.

CXIV. Newbery, Piers. "Superb Federer ends Murray dream." 8 September 2008. BBC Sport. Web.

CXV. Tignor, Steve. "20 for 20 No. 4, Nadal d. Federer, 2009 Australian Open." 18 June 2016. Tennis. Web.

CXVI. Tignor.

CXVII. "Robin Soderling Player Activity." ATP Tour. Web.

CXVIII. "Rafael Nadal Player Activity." ATP Tour. Web.

CXIX. "Rafael Nadal vs. Robin Soderling Head 2 Head." ATP Tour. Web.

CXX. Hodgkinson, Mark. "French Open 2009: Rafael Nadal dumped out by Robin Soderling." 31 May 2009. The Telegraph. Web.

CXXI. "Robin Soderling Player Activity." ATP Tour. Web.

CXXII. Lamont, Tom. "The critical moment." 27 June 2009. The Guardian. Web.

CXXIII. "Roger Federer Player Activity." ATP Tour. Web.

CXXIV. Clarey, Christopher. "The Greatest? Federer's Victory Fills Last Hole on His Resume." 7 June 2009. The New York Times. Web.

CXXV. Riley-Smith. "Rafa Nadal: the real reason I quit Wimbledon in 2009." 17 August 2011. The Week. Web.

CXXVI. "Roger Federer Player Activity." ATP Tour. Web.

CXXVII. "Novak Djokovic Player Activity." ATP Tour. Web.

CXXVIII. "Andy Roddick Player Activity." ATP Tour. Web.

CXXIX.   "Roger Federer vs. Andy Roddick Match Stats Overview." 7 June 2009. ATP Tour. Web.

CXXX. "2009 Wimbledon F: Andy Roddick vs. Roger Federer." 7 June 2009. Tennis Abstract. Web.

CXXXI.   Hodgkinson, Mark. "US Open 2009: Martin del Potro defeats Roger Federer to win first grand slam." 15 September 2009. The Telegraph. Web.

CXXXII.   "Roger Federer Rankings History." ATP Tour. Web.

CXXXIII.   Newbery, Piers. "Roger Federer beats Andy Murray to win Australian Open." 31 January 2010. BBC Sport. Web.

CXXXIV.   "Robin Soderling Player Activity." ATP Tour. Web.

CXXXV.   "Roger Federer vs. Robin Soderling Head 2 Head." ATP Tour. Web.

CXXXVI.   Hodgkinson, Mark. "French Open 2010: Roger Federer left stunned by defeat to Robin Soderling." 1 June 2010. The Telegraph. Web.

CXXXVII.   "Roger Federer Player Activity." ATP Tour. Web.

CXXXVIII.   Mitchell, Kevin. "Novak Djokovic stuns Roger Federer in US Open semi-final." 11 September 2010. The Guardian. Web.

CXXXIX.   "Roger Federer Rankings History." ATP Tour. Web.

CXL.   "Roger Federer Player Activity." ATP Tour. Web.

CXLI.   Mitchell, Kevin. "French Open 2011: Rafael Nadal too hot for great rival Roger Federer." 5 June 2011. The Guardian. Web.

CXLII. Phillips, Brian. "Novak Djokovic: The Shot and the Confrontation." 16 September 2011. Grantland. Web.

CXLIII. Mitchell, Kevin. "US Open 2011: Roger Federer struggles to accept Novak Djokovic defeat." 10 September 2011. The Guardian. Web.

CXLIV.   "Roger Federer Player Activity." ATP Tour. Web.

CXLV. Dirs, Ben. "Wimbledon 2012: Federer comeback denies Benneteau." 29 June 2012. BBC Sport. Web.

CXLVI.   Cambers, Simon. "Wimbledon 2012: Roger Federer beats Novak Djokovic to reach final." 6 July 2012. The Guardian. Web.

CXLVII.   Briggs, Simon. "Wimbledon 2012: Brave Andy Murray succumbs to brilliance of Roger Federer in men's final."

CXLVIII.   "Roger Federer upset in second round." 26 June 2013. ESPN.com. Web.

CXLIX.   Newbery, Piers. "Novak Djokovic beats Roger Federer to win Wimbledon title." 6 July 2014. BBC Sport. Web.

CL.   "Roger Federer Player Activity." ATP Tour. Web.

CLI.   "Federer Opens Up About Knee Surgery." 24 March 2016. ATP Tour. Web.

CLII.   "Roger Federer Player Activity." ATP Tour. Web.

CLIII.   "Roger Federer to miss rest of 2016 season due to knee rehab." 26 July 2016. Sports Illustrated. Web.

CLIV.   "Roger Federer Rankings History." ATP Tour. Web.

CLV. Garber, Greg. "Roger Federer's latest renaissance his most surprising." 24 January 2017. ESPN.com. Web.

CLVI. Gleeson, Michael. "Australian Open 2017: Roger Federer's class undimmed in victory over Jurgen Melzer." 17 January 2017. Sydney Morning Herald. Web.

CLVII. Briggs, Simon, and Eccleshare, Charlie. "Novak Djokovic Stunned by Denis Istomin as six-time Australian Open champion is beaten in five sets." 19 January 2017. The Telegraph. Web.

CLVIII. "Fabulous Federer rolls past Berdych; Now for Nishikori." 20 January 2017. ATP Tour. Web.

CLIX. "Roger Federer vs. Kei Nishikori Head 2 Head." ATP Tour. Web.

CLX. "Australian Open 2017: Roger Federer beats Kei Nishikori to advance to quarter-finals." 22 January 2017. ABC News (Australia). Web.

CLXI. "Mischa Zverev Player Activity." ATP Tour. Web.

CLXII. Trollope, Matt. "Five key moments from Federer v Zverev." 24 January 2017. Australian Open. Web.

CLXIII."Rafael Nadal Player Activity." ATP Tour. Web.

CLXIV. "Roger Federer vs. Stan Wawrinka Head 2 Head." ATP Tour. Web.

CLXV. Rothenberg, Ben. "Roger Federer Beats Stan Wawrinka to Reach Australian Open Final." 26 January 2017. The New York Times. Web.

CLXVI. "Roger Federer vs. Rafael Nadal Head 2 Head." ATP Tour. Web.

CLXVII.	Clarey, Christopher. "Roger Federer, Defying Age, Tops Rafael Nadal in Australian Open Final." 29 January 2017. The New York Times. Web.

CLXVIII.	"Roger Federer opens up on his admiration for Rafael Nadal." 3 January 2017. News.com.au. Web.

CLXIX.	"Roger Federer vs. Rafael Nadal Head 2 Head." ATP Tour. Web.

CLXX. Cutler, Teddy. "Exclusive: How Novak Djokovic's father on how he made his son a multiple grand slam champion." 13 March 2016. Newsweek. Web.

CLXXI.	Cutler.

CLXXII.	"Federer critical of Djokovic." 2009 January 27. ESPN.com. Web.

CLXXIII.	"Roger Federer vs. Novak Djokovic Head 2 Head." ATP Tour. Web.

CLXXIV.	Devgan, Arjun. "Roger Federer and Rafael Nadal open up about Novak Djokovic's recent struggles in tennis." 26 October 2016. International Business Times. Web.

CLXXV.	Perry, Douglas. "Roger Federer vs. Andy Murray: the under-the-radar rivalry." 21 January 2014. The Oregonian/Oregon Live. Web.

CLXXVI.	"Roger Federer vs. Andy Murray Head 2 Head." ATP Tour. Web.

CLXXVII.	Moss, Stephen. "London 2012: Andy Murray holds his nerve to win gold against Roger Federer." 6 August 2012. The Guardian. Web.

CLXXVIII.   "Roger Federer vs. Andy Murray Head 2 Head." ATP Tour. Web.

CLXXIX.   "Roger Federer vs. Stan Wawrinka Head 2 Head." ATP Tour. Web.

CLXXX.   Mitchell, Kevin. "Roger Federer sees off fellow Swiss Stanislas Wawrinka to make ATP final." 15 November 2014. The Guardian. Web.

CLXXXI.   Briggs, Simon. "Roger Federer's wife Mirka sparked row by heckling Stan Wawrinka." 17 November 2014. The Telegraph. Web.

CLXXXII.   "Roger Federer criticizes umpire for confirming his wife Mirka did heckle Stanislas Wawrinka." 18 November 2014. Ireland Independent. Web.

CLXXXIII.   Ireland Independent.

CLXXXIV.   "Stan Wawrinka Player Activity." ATP Tour. Web.

CLXXXV.   "Miroslava Vavrinec Player Profile." WTA Tour. Web.

CLXXXVI.   Newman, Paul. "Federer's Secret Weapon." 26 June 2009. The Independent. Web.

CLXXXVII.   Newman.

CLXXXVIII.   Jones, Chris. "I am not wrecking Federer, says Mirka." 2004. Evening Standard. Web.

CLXXXIX.   Jones.

CXC.   Jones.

CXCI. Burge, Christian. "She is Roger's Ass." 19 July 2012. Schweizer Illustrierte (translated from German by Google). Web.

CXCII. Clarey, Christopher. "Roger Federer Seeks New Experiences to Sustain His Career." 9 March 2015. The New York Times. Web.

CXCIII. Guthrie, Susannah. "'What is she wearing?' Mirka Federer's outfit confuses Aus Open fans." 27 January 2017. The New Daily. Web.

CXCIV. "Roger Federer: New Balls Please." 2013. Life Beyond Sport. Web.

CXCV. Life Beyond Sport.

CXCVI. "Roger Federer Foundation: Our Mission." RogerFedererFoundation.org. Web.

CXCVII. "Balance sheet as of 31 December 2014." RogerFedererFoundation.org. Web.

CXCVIII. Syed, Matthew. "Federer's resolve makes him peerless." 30 January 2017. The Times. Web.

CXCIX. Gleeson.

CC. Robson, Dougas. "Federer takes on backroom role as power broker." 4 November 2012. USA Today. Web.

CCI. Rothenberg, Ben. "Council Replaces Preisdent in Election That's More than a Popularity Contest." 29 August 2014. The New York Times. Web.

CCII. Bevis, Marianne. "Figurehead Federer leaves Players' Council 'proud to have led by example." 22 June 2014. The Sport Review. Web.

CCIII. Almeida, Chris. "Old Future." 18 November 2016. The Ringer. Web.

CCIV. "Jack Nicklaus Player Overview." PGA Tour. Web.

CCV. "Alexander Zverev Player Overview." ATP Tour. Web.

CCVI. "Kyrgios, Zverev, Edmund Lead Best Next Gen Stars of 2016." ATP Tour. Web.